Pancho Villa

Pancho Villa

Steven O'Brien
Traducción por
Francisca Gonzáles-Arias

CHELSEA HOUSE PUBLISHERS
NEW YORK ■ PHILADELPHIA

CHELSEA HOUSE PUBLISHERS

Director editorial: Richard Rennert
Editor gerente ejecutivo: Karyn Gullen Browne
Jefe de redacción: Robin James
Jefe de fotografías: Adrian G. Allen
Director de arte y diseño: Robert Mitchell
Director de fabricación: Gerald Levine

HISPANOS NOTABLES
Editor Jefe: Philip Koslow

EQUIPO PARA PANCHO VILLA
Editor adjunto: David Carter
Editor de pruebas: Nicole Greenblatt
Assistente de redacción: Annie McDonnell
Diseño: M. Cambraia Magalhaes, Lydia Rivera
Investigación fotográfica: Patricia Burns
Portada: Bradford Brown

Primera edición
1 3 5 7 9 8 6 4 2

Library of Congress Cataloging-in-Publication Data
O'Brien, Steven.
[Pancho Villa. Spanish]
Pancho Villa/Steve O'Brien; traducción por Francisca González-Arias.
p. cm.—(Hispanos notables)
Includes bibliographical references and index.
ISBN 0-7910-3104-7
1. Villa, Pancho, 1878–1923—Juvenile literature. 2. Mexico—History—Revolution, 1910–1920—Juvenile literature. 3. Revolutionaries—Mexico—Biography—Juvenile literature. I. González-Arias, Francisca. II. Title. III. Series.
94-15993
F1234.V630318 1994
CIP
972.08'16—dc20

CONTENIDO

CÉSAR CHÁVEZ
Líder obrero mexicanoamericano

ROBERTO CLEMENTE
Jugador puertorriqueño de béisbol

PLÁCIDO DOMINGO
Cantante español

JUAN GONZÁLEZ
Jugador puertorriqueño de béisbol

GLORIA ESTEFAN
Cantante cubanoamericana

FRIDA KAHLO
Pintora mexicana

PABLO PICASSO
Artista español

DIEGO RIVERA
Pintor mexicano

JUNÍPERO SERRA
Misionero y explorador español

PANCHO VILLA
Revolucionario mexicano

C H E L S E A   H O U S E   P U B L I S H E R S

HISPANOS NOTABLES

Rodolfo Cardona

El idioma español y muchos elementos de las culturas hispánicas son parte integral de la cultura actual de los Estados Unidos como igualmente lo fueron desde los comienzos de esta nación. Algunos de estos elementos provienen directamente de la Península Ibérica; otros, indirectamente, de México, del Caribe, y de los países de la América Central y la América del Sur.

La influencia de las culturas hispánicas en los Estados Unidos ha sido tan sutil que muchas personas no han percibido la profundidad de su impacto. La mayoría reconoce la influencia de la cultura española en los Estados Unidos, pero muchas personas no han llegado a darse cabal cuenta de la gran importancia y larga historia de esa influencia. Eso se debe en parte a que en los Estados Unidos se tiende a juzgar la influencia hispánica sólo en términos estadísticos, en lugar de observar detalladamente el impacto individual que algunos hispanos han tenido en esta cultura.

Por lo tanto, resulta lógico que en los Estados Unidos se adquiera algo más que un conocimiento superficial de los orígenes de estos elementos culturales hispánicos y de que se llegue a comprender mejor cómo estos elementos han llegado a formar parte integral de la sociedad estadounidense.

Existe abundante documentación que prueba que los navegantes españoles fueron los primeros en explorar y colonizar territorios que hoy se conocen con el nombre de los Estados Unidos de América. Es por esta razón que los estudiantes de geografía descubren nombres españoles por todo el mapa de los Estados Unidos. Por ejemplo, al Estrecho de Juan de Fuca se le dió ese nombre en honor al explorador español que primero navegó por el Pacífico en las costas del noroeste. Muchos de los nombres de los estados son de origen español, tales como Arizona (zona árida), Montana (montaña), la Florida (llamado así porque el día en que los exploradores españoles llegaron por primera vez a ese territorio fue un domingo de Pascua Florida), y California (nombre de un país ficticio en una de las primeras y famosas novelas españolas de caballeros andantes, el *Amadís de Gaula*), así como muchos de los nombres, también de origen español, de montañas, ríos, desfiladeros, pueblos y ciudades de los Estados Unidos.

Aparte de los exploradores, muchas otros personajes en la historia de España han contribuido a definir la cultura de los Estados Unidos. Por ejemplo, Alfonso X, también llamado Alfonso el Sabio y rey de España durante el siglo XIII, tal vez sea desconocido para la mayoría de los estadounidenses, pero su labor de codificación de las leyes de España ha tenido gran influencia en la evolución de las leyes de los Estados Unidos, particularmente en las juridicciones del suroeste del país. Por esta razón hay una estatua de este rey en Washington, D.C., en la rotonda de la capital. También el nombre de Diego Rivera tal vez sea desconocido para la mayoría de los estadounidenses, pero puede verse la influencia de este pintor mexicano en las obras comisionadas durante la Gran Depresión y la era del Nuevo Trato de los años treinta que hoy adornan las paredes de los edificios del gobierno en todos los Estados Unidos. En años recientes, la contribución de puertorriqueños, mexicanos, mexicanoamericanos (chicanos) y cubanos en ciudades como Boston, Chicago, Los Angeles, Miami, Minneapolis, Nueva York y San Antonio, ha sido enorme.

La importancia del idioma español en este gran complejo cultural es incalculable. Hay que tener en cuenta que, después del inglés, el español es el idioma occidental que más se habla, tanto dentro de los Estados Unidos como en el resto del mundo. La popularidad del idioma español en el territorio de los Estados Unidos tiene una larga historia.

Aparte de los exploradores españoles del Nuevo Mundo, la gran tradición literaria de España contribuyó a traer el idioma y la cultura española a este continente. El interés por la literatura española en lo que hoy son los Estados Unidos comenzó cuando los inmigrantes ingleses trajeron consigo traducciones de las obras maestras españolas de la Edad de Oro. Ya en el año 1683, en bibliotecas privadas en Filadelfia y Boston existían copias de la primera novela picaresca, *Lazarillo de Tormes;* traducciones de *Los Sueños* de Francisco de Quevedo; y copias de la épica inmortal, fantástica y realista a la vez, *Don Quijote de la Mancha,* del gran escritor español Miguel de Cervantes. Es muy posible que Cotton Mather, el puritano por excelencia, haya leído *Don Quijote* en la versión original española, aunque fuese con objeto de aumentar su vocabulario para escribir *La fe del cristiano en 24 artículos de la Institución de Cristo, enviada a los españoles para que abran sus ojos,* publicado en Boston en 1699.

A través de los años los escritores españoles han tenido gran influencia en la literatura de los Estados Unidos, en novelistas tales como Washington Irving, John Steinbeck, Ernest Hemingway, y hasta en poetas como Henry Wadsworth Longfellow y Archibald MacLeish. La tradición literaria española ha dejado su marca en escritores norteamericanos de renombre como James Fenimore Cooper, Edgar Allan Poe, Walt Whitman, Mark Twain y Herman Melville. En algunos escritores como Willa Cather y Maxwell Anderson, que exploraron temas hispánicos a los que estuvieron expuestos en la región suroeste de los Estados Unidos y México, la influencia fue menos directa pero no menos profunda.

Otras personas menos conocidas pero amantes de la cultura hispánica, tales como maestros, impresores, historiadores y nego-

ciantes entre otros, hicieron también importantes contribuciones
a la difusión de esta cultura en los Estados Unidos. Entre estas
contribuciones, una de las más notables es la de Abiel Smith,
quien legó un número de acciones por valor de $20,000 a
la Universidad de Harvard, de donde se había graduado en
1764, para la creación y mantenimiento de una cátedra de
francés y español. Hacia el año 1819 esa donación ya estaba
produciendo lo suficiente para cubrir los gastos de un profesor.
El filólogo y humanista George Ticknor fue el primero en
ocupar la cátedra Abiel Smith, que fue la primera cátedra
dotada de la Universidad de Harvard. Otras personas ilustres que
han ocupado esa cátedra son los poetas Henry Wadsworth
Longfellow y James Russell Lowell.

Ticknor, profesor y hombre de letras de gran renombre, era
también un ávido coleccionista de libros españoles, y así contribuyó de manera muy special al conocimiento de la cultura
española en los Estados Unidos. Fue responsable de reunir una de
las primeras y más importantes colecciones de libros españoles
para las bibliotecas de Harvard. Tenía además una valiosa colección privada de libros y manuscritos españoles, los que luego
donó a la Biblioteca Pública de Boston.

Con la creación de la cátedra Abiel Smith, cursos de español
y de literatura española formaron parte del programa de estudios
de Harvard. Harvard también llegó a convertirse en la primera
universidad de los Estados Unidos en ofrecer estudios
avanzados en lenguas romances. Paulatinamente otros colegios
y universidades en los Estados Unidos siguieron el ejemplo
de Harvard, y hoy en día se puede estudiar el idioma español
y la cultura hispánica en la mayoría de las universidades de
los Estados Unidos.

Cualquier discusión por breve que sea sobre la influencia
española en los Estados Unidos no estaría completa sin men-
cionar la influencia hispánica en las artes plásticas. Pintores del
calibre de John Singer Sargent, James A. Whistler, Thomas Eakins
y Mary Cassatt exploraron temas españoles y experimentaron

con técnicas españolas. Hoy en día, prácticamente todos los pintores serios de los Estados Unidos han estudiado las obras maestras clásicas de España al igual que las de los grandes pintores españoles del siglo XX: Salvador Dalí, Juan Miró y Pablo Picasso.

Sin embargo, probablemente ha sido la música latina la que ha ejercido más influencia en los Estados Unidos. Dos ejemplos obvios los tenemos en composiciones como *West Side Story,* de Leonard Bernstein, la latinización del *Romeo y Julieta* de Shakespeare en un barrio puertorriqueño de Neuva York; y *Salón México,* de Aaron Copeland. En general, la influencia de los ritmos latinos—del tango al mambo, de la guaracha a la salsa—se perciben en prácticamente cualquier forma de música en los Estados Unidos.

Esta serie de biografías que Chelsea House ha publicado bajo el título general HISPANOS NOTABLES, representa un reconocimiento más de la contribución de las culturas hispánicas no sólo en los Estados Unidos sino en todo el mundo civilizado, así como también un renovado esfuerzo por difundir entre la juventud de los Estados Unidos el alcance de esta contribución. Los hombres y las mujeres a quienes se dedican los volúmenes de esta serie han tenido gran éxito en sus respectivos campos y han dejado una marca indeleble en la sociedad estadounidense.

El título de esta serie debe considerarse de la forma más amplia posible. Por *hispanos* deben de entenderse españoles, hispanoamericanos, y personas de otros países cuyo idioma y cultura tienen origen español, ya sea directa o indirectamente. Los nombres de muchas de las personas incluidas en esta serie son muy conocidos; otros lo son menos. Sin embargo, todos se han distinguido en sus patrias respectivas y, en muchos casos, su fama es internacional.

La serie HISPANOS NOTABLES se refiere a los éxitos y a las luchas de hispanos en los Estados Unidos y trata de personas cuya vidas privadas o profesionales reflejan la experiencia hispánica en un sentido más general. Estas historias ejemplifican lo que el ser humano puede lograr frente a grandes dificultades, haciendo enormes sacrificios personales, cuando tienen convicción y determinación.

Fray Junípero Serra, el misionero franciscano español del siglo XVIII, es uno de esos personajes. A pesar de no haber gozado de buena salud, dedicó los últimos quince años de su vida a fundar misiones en California, por aquella época un territorio vasto pero poco habitado, a fin de lograr una vida mejor para los americanos nativos, enseñándoles artesanías y la cría de animales domésticos a los habitantes nativos. Un ejemplo de los tiempos actuales es César Chávez, líder obrero mexicanoamericano que ha luchado contra una oposición enconada, haciendo toda clase de sacrificios personales para ayudar a obreros del sector agrícola que han sido explotados por décadas en las plantaciones del suroeste del país.

Los hombres y mujeres de estas historias han tenido que dedicar gran esfuerzo y mucho trabajo para desarrollar sus talentos innatos y hacerlos florecer. Muchos han disfrutado en vida del éxito en sus labores, otros han muerto pobres y olvidados. Algunos llegaron a su meta sólo después de muchos años de esfuerzo, otros han disfrutado del éxito desde temprano, y para algunos la lucha no ha terminado. Todos ellos, sin embargo, han dejado su marca, y debemos reconocer sus éxitos en el presente así como en el futuro.

Pancho Villa

BANDOLERO

A principios de noviembre de 1913, después de tres días de combate encarnizado pero no decisivo, le quedaban pocas opciones al revolucionario mexicano Pancho Villa. No había más remedio que ordenar parar el asalto a la ciudad de Chihuahua. Las tropas federales que estaban defendiendo Chihuahua estaban demasiado bien armadas y atrincheradas para ser desalojadas por los rebeldes de su División del Norte.

Tan pronto como las patrullas federales de reconocimiento informaron que todas las tropas de Villa habían dejado la zona de Chihuahua, todos los generales del dictador mexicano Victoriano Huerta suspiraron en señal de alivio. La atrevida jugada de Villa de recuperar su posición como uno de los principales líderes rebeldes con la toma de Chihuahua había fracasado. Ahora, pensaban que era una cuestión de días antes de que fuera capturado y ejecutado.

Desaparecida la amenaza de un asalto villista, la vida en el norte de México volvió a la normalidad. El telégrafo volvió a funcionar y se reanudó el servicio de ferrocarril.

Pero la noticia de la desaparición de Villa era prematura. Su decisión de ordenar una retirada al desierto no significaba que había sido derrotado. Cuando sus agentes interceptaron un mensaje tele-

Francisco "Pancho" Villa, fotografiado durante los primeros años de la Revolución Mexicana cuando dirigía las fuerzas rebeldes en el norte de México. Para algunos un malvado, para otros un héroe, Villa dejó una huella indeleble en la historia y el folklore de México.

15

gráfico detallando el horario de un tren que llevaba
carbón al sur de Ciudad Juárez, la ciudad fronteriza
más importante de México, Villa se dió cuenta de que
el destino le había deparado una oportunidad que por
nada de este mundo debía dejar pasar por alto. Pronto
formuló un plan arriesgado para sacar partido de la
excesiva confianza de sus contrarios. La posibilidad de
una catástrofe era tremenda, pero Villa no vaciló. Sabía
que tenía que aceptar todos los riesgos necesarios para
poder volver a tomar la iniciativa.

En una cuestión de horas, Villa había seleccionado
2,000 de sus mejores soldados para ir con él, los cuales
iniciaron una marcha forzada a un lugar estratégico a
través del desierto al sur de Ciudad Juárez por donde
pasaba el ferrocarril.

Organizar la emboscada de un tren era un asunto
sencillo para el antiguo ladrón de trenes. Se levantó
una barricada que atravesaba la vía por un estrecho
desfiladero, y cuando el tren se detuvo, Villa y sus
hombres bajaron de los cañones y derrotaron a la
escolta militar que estaba a bordo. Cuando el tren
incautado hizo su última parada para reabastecerse de
combustible antes de llegar a Chihuahua, los rebeldes
se apoderaron de la oficina de telégrafos de la estación.

Los villistas encañonaron la cabeza del telegrafista
y le obligaron a transmitir un mensaje a Juárez. Le
indicaron que uno de ellos sabía el sistema Morse
y que cualquier intento de avisar a las guarniciones
en Juárez o en Chihuahua daría como resultado una
muerte rápida. Villa ordenó que se enviara el siguiente
mensaje: DESCARRILADO. NO HAY VÍA A CHI-
HUAHUA. LOS REVOLUCIONARIOS QUE-
MARON TODO. ENVIEN SEGUNDO MOTOR
Y ÓRDENES. Después de un tenso y breve momento, llegó la respuesta de Ciudad Juárez: NO HAY
MOTORES. BUSQUEN HERRAMIENTAS. AV-
ISEN Y ESPEREN ÓRDENES CUANDO VUEL-
VAN A LA VÍA.

Villa y algunos de sus oficiales vestidos para la batalla. Las osadas tácticas militares de Villa, desarrolladas cuando era un líder bandolero, permitieron a su División del Norte a derrotar a las fuerzas federales, más numerosas y mejor armadas, en 1913.

En dos horas, el tren se había vaciado de su depósito de carbón y ahora llevaba un cargamento muy diferente, 2,000 revolucionarios villistas. Villa entonces le ordenó al telegrafista que enviara un segundo telegrama: EN LA VÍA. NO HAY NI CAMINO NI TELÉGRAFO AL SUR. GRAN NUBE DE POLVO. QUIZÁS REVOLUCIONARIOS. Inmediatamente los cables empezaron a zumbar con la respuesta: VUELVAN A JUÁREZ. TELEGRAFIEN DESDE CADA ESTACIÓN. Villa les ordenó a sus hombres que cortaran el cable de telégrafos para que no se pudiera avisar después de que los revolucionarios se hubieran marchado. Otros, rápidamente, rompieron los ráiles hacia el sur para hacer imposible que se les viniera persiguiendo desde Chihuahua.

Mientras que el tren en su camino hacia el norte llegaba a cada estación, los telegrafistas eran obligados a enviar las requeridas señales "todo bien" a Juárez. Cuando los rebeldes se acercaban a la ciudad, Villa colocó a varios de sus hombres y uno de sus ferroviarios en la máquina del tren y emitió estas rigurosas órdenes: Si el maquinista intentaba parar antes de llegar a la estación "mátenlo, apoderénse de los mandos, y mantengan el tren en movimiento."

Cuatro horas después de incautarse del tren, Villa penetraba en la ciudad fuertemente fortificada sin que nadie se percatara de su peligroso cargamento. Antes de que se pudiera sonar una alarma, los rebeldes desfilaron de los vagones del tren y se desplegaron para capturar los lugares estratégicos de Juárez.

La sorpresa fue total. Los 4,000 soldados federales, totalmente dormidos cuando el tren de Villa entraba estruendosamente en la ciudad, estaban todos tan asombrados por el asalto de los rebeldes que el 15 de noviembre al amanecer, los villistas o bien habían matado, o bien capturado, o bien inducido a la fuga a casi toda la guarnición. Aunque esta hazaña destacaba solamente por su osadía, el astuto líder revolucionario había tomado Ciudad Juárez por una importante razón estratégica: era la línea vital a Chihuahua, el único reducto importante del gobierno méxicano en el norte. Si Villa podía controlar el ferrocarril entre las dos ciudades, podría él aportar de forma significativa a la Revolución Mexicana expulsando al gobierno federal del norte de México.

Al parecer, los enemigos de Villa compartían su punto de vista sobre la situación. Pocos días después de capturar Ciudad Juárez, Villa supo que 11 trenes cargados de tropas federales venían velozmente rumbo al norte desde la ciudad de Chihuahua. Villa se dirigió a

Soldados rebeldes disparan contra las fuerzas federalistas durante la batalla de Ciudad Juárez en noviembre de 1913. Después de penetrar furtivamente en Ciudad Juárez por tren mientras dormía la guarnición federalista, los villistas rápidamente se apoderaron de la importante ciudad y pronto procedieron a la conquista de Chihuahua.

uno de los comandantes en que más confiaba, Rodolfo Fierro, y le mandó ganar a cualquier precio un día para los rebeldes. Fierro partió en seguida con un destacamento y volvió pocas horas después anunciando que había cumplido con éxito su misión. Aunque estaban al alcance de la artillería federal, Fierro y sus hombres habían inutilizado la vía del tren. Y como toque adicional, habían dejado 10 vagones de tren ardiendo en los raíles.

Al día siguiente, Villa y su ejército partieron para luchar contra los federales. Esta vez, el líder de los rebeldes estaba preocupado no sólo por cuestiones militares. En 1911, en una batalla en Ciudad Juárez, la contienda se había esparcido al otro lado de la frontera a la ciudad de El Paso en tierras tejanas, provocando la cólera de los ciudadanos. Para evitar que se repitiera el enfado de los Estados Unidos, Villa se reunió con el alcalde de El Paso inmediatamente después de apod-

erarse de Ciudad Juárez, y prometió no volver a repetir
el incidente anterior.

Como era su costumbre, Villa supo cómo sacar
partido de este problema diplomático. El 16 de
noviembre, ordenó un desfile impresionante de sus
tropas con el doble propósito de celebrar el aniver-
sario de la Revolución Mexicana y de asegurar a los
ciudadanos de El Paso que todo estaba bajo su control.
Cuando el defile se había terminado, las tropas de Villa
no volvieron al cuartel como era esperado, sino que se

Los villistas a punto de montar en tren en noviembre de 1913. Antiguo ladrón de trenes, Villa conocía los pormenores de los ferrocarriles mexicanos. Su capacidad de movilizar rápidamente a tropas y provisiones le permitió conquistar el norte de México para la revolución.

montaron en trenes que aguardaban y salieron hacia el sur. Villa ya había decidido encontrarse con las fuerzas federales que avanzaban por Tierra Blanca, 35 millas al sur de Juárez. Pensaba ocupar la tierra alta, obligando al enemigo a luchar en un terreno arenoso que inmovilizaría su artillería y les privaría de agua.

Cuando los ejércitos se encontraron en Tierra Blanca, los contrarios de Villa comprendieron que les había atrapado. Al principio no atacaron, esperando posiblemente que Villa abandonara su posición superior y que luchara en el terreno de ellos. Cuando Villa no les complació, se vieron obligados el 22 de noviembre a atacarle por el lado derecho, esperando tomar la estación de ferrocarril de Bauche y sus importantísimas reservas de agua en cisternas. Tuvo lugar una batalla campal, pero las fuerzas villistas se mantuvieron firmes.

Al día siguiente, el 23 de noviembre, los federales atacaron el lado izquierdo de Villa y fracasaron de nuevo en su tentativa de penetración. Mientras sus provisiones de agua seguían disminuyendo, las tropas de Villa se beneficiaban de la comprensión, por parte de su comandante, del uso militar del ferrocarril; recibían no sólo agua, sino también alimentos y medicinas de Ciudad Juárez. Para el 25 de noviembre, el fragor de la batalla casi rozaba la frontera con Tejas. Los federales lanzaron un último y desesperado intento de romper las líneas villistas y casi consiguieron el triunfo. En el momento más crítico, Villa decidió emplear una de sus maniobras preferidas: una carga masiva de caballería embistiendo al mismo centro del enemigo. Les informó a sus oficiales que la señal para el ataque sería el disparo de dos cañones.

Cuando los disparos de los cañones rompieron el caldeado aire que cubría Tierra Blanca, la caballería veloz de los rebeldes desgarró las líneas federales como si fueran llamas arrasando un campo de trigo. Soldados paralizados de pánico huyeron del campo de batalla e intentaron alcanzar Chihuahua en tren. Muchos se escaparon, pero algunos no fueron tan afortunados. Uno de los trenes fue interceptado por el temible Rodolfo Fierro: saltó de su caballo a bordo del tren, trepando por los techos de los vagones hasta alcanzar el cilindro de los frenos, haciendo que el tren se detuviera de repente. Los villistas atacaron a los ocupantes del tren y se dice que hasta el propio Villa reconoció que tuvo lugar una matanza terrible.

Después de Tierra Blanca se daba por hecho que Villa tomaría finalmente la ciudad de Chihuahua, encabezando así la revolución en el norte de México. Era extraordinario que sólo algo más de diez meses antes, Villa había cruzado la frontera de Tejas con sólo ocho seguidores. Su único propósito entonces era vengar el asesinato de su ídolo, el presidente mexicano Francisco Madero y de ayudar a salvar la revolución méxicana. El hombre que había sido una vez un campesino humilde y después un bandido infame triunfó de tal forma que, al llegar a Tierra Blanca, una revista influyente de los Estados Unidos se había referido a la revolución como "el levantamiento de Villa."

Debido a sus asombrosas victorias frente a condiciones desfavorables, la gente de los estados del norte de México, Chihuahua, Durango y Sonora aún cuentan historias de las hazañas de Pancho Villa. Al norte del Río Grande se le recuerda más bien como un criminal.

Los dos puntos de vista contienen elementos de la verdad. Pancho Villa era capaz de desenfreno, de auto-sacrificio patriótico, de mutilación brutal, y de honda generosidad. Para poder entender los impulsos antagónicos de su naturaleza, es necesario comprender el mundo violento que lo formó.

BANDIDO PATRIOTA

F rancisco "Pancho" Villa nació en el pueblo pequeño de Río Grande en Durango, estado del norte de México, el 5 de junio de 1878. Fue bautizado como Doroteo Arango. Los padres de Doroteo, Agustín Arango y María Micaela Arámbula, eran campesinos analfabetos que trabajaban de sol a sol en una gran propiedad conocida como la Hacienda del Río Grande.

La instrucción escolar de Doroteo consistió sólo en las primeras letras que aprendió en la pequeña escuela del pueblo regida por la iglesia. A la edad de siete años, cuando murió su padre, tuvo que ayudar a cuidar de sus hermanos y hermanas más jóvenes. A los 11 años, había logrado combinar su amor por los caballos y su necesidad de suplir los escasos ingresos de la familia: obtuvo un trabajo como ayudante de carretero. Este trabajo le permitió escaparse de los confines del aislado pueblo rural donde vivía. Más importante aún para el futuro bandido y líder revolucionario fue que le proporcionó un conocimiento íntimo del desierto y del terreno montañoso del norte de México.

Doroteo era un adolescente popular y muy respetado en su pueblo, pero tenía un carácter demasiado fuerte y era demasiado trabajador para aceptar

Pancho Villa cuando tenía veinte y pico años, poco después de ser nombrado general del ejército revolucionario. Bandido desde la edad de 16 años, Villa halló en la Revolución Mexicana una salida para su odio de toda la vida contra los ricos terratenientes mexicanos.

mansamente la vida humilde de un jornalero. Cuando surgió una oportunidad para ganar más dinero trabajando en la Hacienda del Norte, la aceptó sin obtener el permiso del dueño de la Hacienda del Río Grande.

La acción de Doroteo era contra la ley. En el México del siglo XIX, el castigo por un comportamiento tan independiente por parte de un peón era salvaje. Doroteo fue capturado, atado y obligado a correr descalzo detrás de un caballo todo el camino de vuelta a la Hacienda del Norte. Después, en la plaza mayor de Río Grande, fue azotado brutalmente. El dolor agudísimo y la humillación que sufrió intensificó el espíritu rebelde del muchacho. Empezó a asociarse con el líder de un grupo de jóvenes de quienes se sospechaba eran ladrones de ganado. Después de un nuevo intento fracasado de escaparse de la hacienda, fue declarado culpable de ser cómplice en el hurto y la muerte de una res robada. Después de un juicio rápido Doroteo, que tenía 16 años, fue condenado a la cárcel.

Doroteo fue soltado después de unos pocos meses, gracias a los esfuerzos del dueño de una hacienda vecina. Pero la experiencia de vivir en una celda inmunda entre criminales endurecidos le afectó profundamente. En lugar de volver directamente a su pueblo, Doroteo obtuvo trabajos humildes en la ciudad de Chihuahua. Al parecer también cultivó los contactos con el mundo del hampa que había adquirido en la prisión. Para ganar un poco más de dinero, les pasaba información que obtenía de los cargamentos de oro y los traslados de ganado.

El dinero que ganaba en Chichuahua le permitía a Doroteo ayudar a mantener a su familia. También tenía suficiente tiempo y recursos para cortejar a una joven indígena llamada María Luz Corral. Se enamoraron y se comprometieron.

Doroteo pudo haber sido jornalero y ratero por el resto de sus días si no se hubiera visto obligado a

Jornaleros mexicanos aran la tierra a principios del siglo XX, usando métodos milenarios. Villa nació en esta oprimida clase rural, pero por su naturaleza rebelde llegó a ser un atrevido proscrito sin escrúpulos.

vengàr el honor de su hermana menor. Cuando supo que el hijo de un hacendado la había seducido y abandonado, se enfrentó a él y le disparó, causando su muerte. El castigo por agredir a un aristócrata, por la razón que fuera, era la muerte. Doroteo no tuvo más alternativa que robar el caballo más veloz y huir a las montañas remotas conocidas como la Sierra Madre.

Frente a innumerables circunstancias desfavorables, el joven fugitivo logró evadir a todas las patrullas de policía enviadas en su búsqueda. Ya tenía la experiencia de ocultar sus huellas y conservar la fuerza de su caballo evitando la tentación de escaparse corriendo a toda velocidad. El adolescente conocía los mejores escondites en el áspero terreno montañoso, el tipo de cactus que se podía partir para conseguir la indispensable humedad y el arte de fabricar trampas silenciosas para cazar liebres y armadillos, que se podían comer crudos para alimentarse.

Un mañana, después de pasar la noche al lado de un riachuelo en un cañón verdoso de la Barranca del Cobre, Doroteo se despertó sobresaltado. Le estaba mirando fijamente el infame bandolero, Ignacio Parra.

Parra era el hombre al que el muchacho deseaba conocer, pero tuvo que depender de su ingenio para lograr el derecho de unirse a su banda. Para comprobar su mérito potencial, dibujó mapas en la arena ilustrando los diferentes lugares de pasto de varias de las manadas de ganado más grandes de la región. Parra quedó tan impresionado por el aguante y el ingenio que Doroteo había mostrado al escaparse de la policía que decidió arriesgarse con él. Al cabo de unos meses, el muchacho era un miembro, con todos sus derechos, de la banda de Parra.

Junto con su nueva vida, Doroteo escogió un nuevo nombre—Francisco "Pancho" Villa. El Pancho Villa original había sido un conocido líder de bandoleros que, según la leyenda, robaba de los ricos y ayudaba a los pobres. Doroteo estaba convencido de que su destino era hacer lo mismo. Tenía un pariente lejano llamado Jesús Villa, y pensaba que ésto establecía un vínculo entre él y el bandido legendario.

Doroteo no sólo había cambiado su nombre, sino que se había convertido en un hombre con un pecho como un tonel, y unos rizados cabellos castaños rojizos. Se dejó crecer un bigote tupido para ocultar su dentadura desigual y prominente que daba la impresión que llevaba una sonrisa permanente. Ancho de espaldas, de casi dos metros de altura; llamaba la atención al lado de sus compatriotas méxicanos.

Villa generalmente era reservado y autodisciplinado, pero tenía muy mal genio y el motivo más insignificante lo podía hacer estallar. Cualquier hombre que frustraba sus deseos, que le engañaba o le insultaba era afortunado si se escapaba con sólo una buena paliza. Villa nunca olvidaba una traición y siempre se vengaba.

Después de unirse a la banda de Parra, Villa participó en muchos asaltos a haciendas y robó innumerables cabezas de ganado. Además de convertirse en un criminal sin escrúpulos, capaz de asesinar y torturar sin piedad, aprendió a ser un hábil jinete, tirador y táctico. Su extraordinaria capacidad de liderazgo y de inspirar lealtad surgió primero entre los bandidos de Chihuahua.

En la técnica de asalto que Parra acostumbraba emplear, los bandidos se acercaban cautelosamente a su meta en plena noche. Al amanecer se arrojaban en medio de una tempestad de gritos y disparos. Cuando todo salía según el plan previsto, las víctimas eran despojadas de sus mercancías y efectos personales en pocos minutos. Entonces, los bandoleros volvían rápidamente a los cañones de la Sierra Madre, eludiendo, en el escarpado terreno montañoso, a la policía que venía en su búsqueda.

Un día, los bandidos cayeron en una trampa mortal urdida por las tropas federales; asaltaron un vagón que transportaba jornales, y que servía de señuelo. Parra fue asesinado en un tiroteo, y los bandoleros sin jefe empezaron a aterrarse. Villa salvó la situación animando a los sobrevivientes y dirigiendo una carga desesperada que les permitió escaparse.

De vuelta en su escondite, el grupo diezmado aceptó formalmente a Villa como el sucesor de Parra. Villa pronto concibió un nuevo modo de operación para la banda. A los que no eran conocidos por la policía, se les ordenó que volvieran a la vida civil. Mientras tanto, Villa y un pequeño cuerpo de hombres permanecieron en las montañas para llevar a cabo espionaje y planear asaltos. Cuando se acercaba el momento de un asalto se enviaba a un jinete por la noche. El grito "¡Viva Villa!"—acompañado de un puñal clavado en la puerta de la casa de adobe— era la señal citándole a un lugar fijado previamente, listo para participar en un asalto.

A diferencia de algunos de sus compañeros, Villa no era un criminal de carrera. En los años entre su ingreso en la banda de Parra y el estallido de la revolución en 1910, hizo varios intentos de incorporarse a la sociedad convencional. Una vez, por una breve temporada, trabajó como jornalero en el sur de Arizona y en Nuevo México. En 1903, aceptó la oportunidad de ser amnistiado presentándose como "voluntario" para prestar servicio en el 14 Regimento de Caballería. Cuando María Luz Corral y él se casaron legalmente en 1909, compró una casa grande y cómoda en la ciudad de Chihuahua.

A pesar del deseo repetido de echar raíces, la vida de líder de bandoleros era demasiado emocionante y económicamente provechosa para cambiarla por la tranquilidad doméstica. Sólo viviendo al márgen de la ley podía Villa satisfacer su pasión por las mujeres sin hacer caso de las convenciones sociales tradicionales. Además de María Luz, se casó por lo menos con otras dos mujeres, Soledad Seáñez y Estroberta Rentería, mantuvo a varias amantes, y tuvo innumerables romances fugaces.

Hasta cierta medida, las condiciones sociales de México a finales del siglo XIX condujeron a hombres como Villa al bandolerismo. En México, como en los Estados Unidos, ésta fue la época del *robber baron* (señor feudal que vivía del robo), los capitalistas que se enriquecieron por medios ilegales. Prevalecía la mentalidad de la "supervivencia del más apto," sin que la mitigara la idea de compartir la riqueza nacional con esos menos capaces de competir. De forma sistemática, la política económica de Porfirio Díaz, el dictador de México, conducía a la ruina y casi a la esclavitud a los pequeños agricultores y estancieros.

Díaz gobernó México de 1877 a 1911. Su política principal era de atraer capital extranjero a Mexico. Pronto los europeos y los norteamericanos eran los dueños de terrenos extensos, las compañías mineras y los ferrocarriles. El dinero afluía al país, pero la riqueza obtenida por una pequeña minoría de mexicanos nunca descendía a la gran mayoría de la población.

Porfirio Díaz, presidente de México de 1877 a 1911. Un dictador autoritario,
Díaz intentó fomentar la economía de México dando facilidades a ricos
terratenientes y a empresarios extranjeros. Su política fue la causa directa de
la Revolución Mexicana de 1910.

Díaz abolió las salvaguardas que habían controlado la avaricia de los ricos. El pequeño hacendado era una cosa del pasado. En su lugar surgieron propietaros que vivían fuera; adquirían haciendas inmensas y pagaban a administradores para que se las llevaran, con la única meta de sacar las máximas ganancias posibles.

La temida policía de Díaz, llamada los Rurales, controlaba la población por medio de la brutalidad y el terror. Se les autorizaba a los Rurales, que originalmente se reclutaban de los bandidos capturados que eran amnistiados si se unían al cuerpo, a disparar contra delincuentes y revolucionarios, en lugar de llevarlos a juicio. Era probable que a los peones esca-

Durante su presidencia, Díaz creó los Rurales— fotografiados aquí con un grupo de rebeldes muertos—para aterrorizar a los campesinos y aplastar a sus adversarios políticos.

pados, los obreros en huelga, y a los enemigos personales y los rivales de los caciques locales se les ejecutara por "intentar fugarse." Lo que los Rurales no podían controlar, lo solucionaba el ejército. Díaz mantenía la lealtad de los oficiales del ejército y de la iglesia por medio del soborno y la concesión de privilegios especiales.

En este ambiente, los hombres de orígen humilde que recurrían a la delincuencia eran percebidos por las masas como héroes que luchaban en contra de la opresión. Muchos romances y leyendas populares surgieron sobre Villa. Estas canciones y anécdotas míticas exageraban sus hazañas de bandolero y sostenían que él, como la persona cuyo nombre había tomado, ayudaban a los pobres con los despojos de los ricos.

La vida de Villa antes de 1910 le proporcionó un aprendizaje ideal para el papel de guerrillero consumado. La preparación y la ejecución de robos de trenes, de bancos y de asaltos a haciendas le obligaron a ser autosuficiente, a eludir a los que lo perseguían, a dominar a hombres revoltosos y a coordinar asaltos sorpresa. Lo único que le hacía falta para cambiar de bandido a patriota era una ideología revolucionaria que encauzara su rabia y un líder al que pudiera seguir. En el verano y el otoño de 1910, halló su inspiración.

En 1908, Díaz le dijo a un periodista norteamericano que México estaba listo para la democracia. Esta declaración ocasionó un brote de actividad política por parte de las fuerzas contra Díaz. *La sucesión presidencial en 1910,* un libro de Francisco Indalécio Madero, se convirtió en un éxito inmediato. Pedía elecciones legítimas en 1910, instituciones democráticas a todos los niveles del gobierno y la derrota de Díaz. Además de sus elocuentes escritos políticos, Madero también intentó organizar a todos los diferentes grupos que se oponían al régimen prolongado de Díaz en un partido Antireeleccionista.

Madero obtuvo mucho más apoyo popular de lo que Díaz había previsto cuando le había concedido el permiso para hacer campaña electoral. Tan pronto como se hizo claro de que había la posibilidad de que perdiera las elecciones de 1910, Díaz ordenó el encarcelamiento de Madero y le obligó a Abrán González, el candidato para vicepresidente, a huir a los Estados Unidos. Después de volver a ser reeligido en unas elecciones fraudulentas, Díaz soltó a Madero, advirtiéndole que debía permanecer callado. En lugar de aceptar la derrota, Madero reanudó sus protestas y se escapó a San Antonio, Tejas. En octubre de 1910, publicó *El plan de San Luis Potosí,* un manifiesto que prometía la revisión de todas las leyes promulgadas durante el régimen de Díaz. Se declaró a si mismo presidente legítimo de México e hizo un llamamiento por una insurrección armada para derrocar a Díaz. La Revolución Mexicana había empezado.

La oportunidad de eludir la vida de fugitivo y de jugar un papel en el futuro de Mexico le resultó irresistible a Villa. El 15 de noviembre, 1910, a la cabeza de un grupo de 15 hombres, volvió a las montañas que conocía tan bien, no como bandido, sino como capitán del ejército revolucionario.

La Revolución Mexicana no fue el resultado de un movimiento de oposición bien coordinado. En vez de una rebelión, había varias, en muchas partes diferentes de México. Cada rebelión tenía su propio líder, programa y zona de influencia. Por unos pocos meses, Madero era el líder titular de una organización revolucionaria que abarcaba a varios grupos, pero nunca controló firmemente a más de un pequeño número de seguidores leales.

Mientras Madero se esforzaba por crear una organización nacional, Villa, a la cabeza de 500 hombres, capturó el importante empalme ferroviario de Camargo. Las reglas del comportamiento que impuso en ambas comunidades—prohibiendo la violación y

Francisco Indalecio Madero (1873–1913) era un rico hacendista que llegó a ser un reformador social y el líder de la oposición contra Díaz. El valor y el idealismo de Madero, atrajeron la admiración de Villa, que se puso a sí mismo y a sus bandidos bajo las órdenes de Madero en 1910.

el pillaje, la ejecución de todos los oficiales militares enemigos capturados, además de la colección de un impuesto especial a los comerciantes locales, "préstamos" forzados de dueños extranjeros de minas para obtener el dinero para equipar a su ejército—fueron las mismas que intentó seguir a lo largo de la mayor parte de su carrera militar.

En marzo de 1911 el ejército revolucionario, con Madero a la cabeza, sufrió una derrota aplastante en la batalla de Casas Grandes en Chihuahua. Sin embargo, Madero obtuvo la admiración de Villa cuando siguió luchando valientemente después de sufrir una herida grave en el hombro.

Después de la derrota, Madero reunió a todas las fuerzas rebeldes que aún le seguían y Villa se presentó a su servicio con un ejército de 800 hombres. Le dieron la tarea de cubrir la retirada de los rebeldes a la zona de Ciudad Juárez.

La batalla de Casas Grandes hizo creer erróneamente a los observadores extranjeros y a los generales de Díaz que el gobierno había aplastado la reunión. En realidad, aunque la derrota había disminuido su ejército, Madero contaba aún con una fuerza más disciplinada y mejor equipada que nunca. También adoptó un objetivo militar más realístico—capturar el importante centro fronterizo de Ciudad Juárez. Controlar Juárez les permitiría a los rebeldes tener acceso a armas y a la ayuda económica de los Estados Unidos.

Los detalles de la toma de Juárez el 10 de mayo de 1911 no están claros, pero el valor, la energía y la iniciativa de Villa fueron los ingredientes vitales de la victoria decisiva. Jugó un papel principal en el desarrollo del plan de ataque, llevó a cabo varias cargas durante los cuatro días que duró la batalla, y concibió una estrategia sencilla para superar las barricadas callejeras aparentemente impenetrables de la guarnición federal. En lugar de malgastar a hombres en un asalto directo a las barricadas, Villa—familiarizado, por su carrera de ladrón de bancos, con la vulnerabilidad de los edificios de madera o de adobe frente a la dinamita—mandó a sus hombres colocar explosivos en los edificios de un lado de una calle barricada. De esta manera, se abrió un camino a través de las casas que rodeaban las barricadas. Los defensores, cuyo flanco había sido desbordado, eran obligados a rendirse o a retirarse a la siguiente barricada, donde correrían la misma suerte.

Cuando se rindió el General Juan Navarro, comandante de la guarnición federal, Madero estableció un gobierno provisional. Aunque Villa fue ascendido a coronel por su actuación durante la batalla, la negativa de Madero a la ejecución de los oficiales enemigos

Rebeldes mexicanos en Cuidad Juárez. La captura de Juárez en mayo de 1911, después del ataque planeado por Villa, fue un desastre para el régimen Díaz.

capturados le incomodó casi tanto como el nombramiento de Giuseppe Garibaldi, el nieto del patriota italiano del siglo XIX, como su guardaespaldas personal. Garibaldi era el comandante de la Legión Americana, un grupo de soldados mercenarios europeos y americanos que se habían unido al ejército revolucionario. Una noche poco después de la batalla, Villa y él tuvieron una discusión tan violenta que Villa siguió a Garibaldi hasta el otro lado del Río Grande en El Paso, Tejas, para retarle a un duelo. En lugar de obtener la satisfacción deseada, Villa sufrió la indignidad de ser desarmado por oficiales norteamericanos y escoltado de vuelta al lado méxicano de la frontera.

Pascual Orozco, un oficial rebelde, decepcionado por no haber sido nombrado ministro de guerra en el gabinete de Madero, sacó provecho de la frustración de Villa. Le persuadió a que se uniera a él y a varios centenares de sus tropas más leales para ir a quejarse directamente a Madero. En la reunión en el cuartel general de Madero, Orozco sorprendió a Villa al exigir que Madero aceptara la custodia protectiva de ambos.

Madero no se dejó intimidar, aunque su sede estaba rodeada por tropas leales a Orozco y a Villa. Escuchó cortesmente las quejas de ellos, expresó su simpatía, les explicó las razones que motivaron las acciones de él, y prometió que en el futuro tendría presente el servicio que prestaron a la revolución.

La respuesta de Madero complació a Villa. Tan pronto como anunció que no había acudido a la reunión con ninguna intención de usurpar la autoridad de Madero, Orozco en seguida concurrió.

El incidente tuvo importantes resultados a largo plazo. La firmeza de Madero y su valor personal durante la tensa confrontación transformó los sentimientos de Villa hacia él de una aceptación vacilante a una dedicación total y absoluta. Sus sentimientos

Un grupo de rebeldes mexicanos ocupa una plaza fuerte en las montañas de Chihuahua. En la distancia, al otro lado de la frontera, una sección industrial de El Paso, Tejas.

hacia Orozco pasaron de la indiferencia a un odio violento. Estaba convencido de que Orozco le había engañado para que se enfrentara a Madero creando así la impresión de que Villa era el instigador de lo que en realidad era la traición de Orozco.

La victoria inesperada de Madero en Juárez y el levantamiento exitoso del líder campesino Emiliano Zapata en el sur de México condujo al rápido desmoronamiento del régimen de Díaz. El 21 de mayo de 1911, sólo 11 días después de la toma de Juárez, Díaz anunció su decisión de renunciar a la presidencia. Varios días después, Madero, acompañado de sus ministros y oficiales militares, incluyendo a Villa, llegó a ciudad de México para asumir el mando del país.

Ya que parecía que la guerra se había terminado, Villa pidió, y se le concedió, permiso para dejar el ejército revolucionario y volver a la ciudad de Chihuahua. En compensación por sus servicios, fue autorizado a confiscar el ganado de don Luis Terrazas, un partidario de Díaz y un hacendista a quien Villa odiaba con una pasión particular. Villa necesitaba el ganado para abastecer a varias carnicerías con refrigeración moderna que proyectaba abrir en la ciudad de Chihuahua.

Durante los próximos meses, Villa estaba completamente envuelto en el desarrollo de su nuevo negocio. Este fue uno de los pocos períodos de su vida de adulto durante el cual, aunque con una desequilibrada ventaja sobre sus competidores, tenía un trabajo legítimo. Para celebrar su buena fortuna y el nacimiento de un segundo hijo, volvió a casarse con María Luz ambos por la iglesia y por lo civil; ofreció a centenares de invitados una gigantesca barbacoa y a una recepción.

Sin embargo, su destino no iba a ser el de hombre de negocios.

EL FUGITIVO

Francisco Madero fue elegido presidente de México por una mayoría sobrecogedora en octubre de 1911. Entró en funciones el 6 de noviembre y fue aclamado a lo largo de México como "el apóstol de la democracia." Desafortunadamente, la esperanza de que Madero pudiera establecer un gobierno viable consagrado a la reforma moderada y gradual pronto se desvaneció. Antiguos aliados como Pascual Orozco y Bernardo Reyes pronto le traicionaron para prosperar personalmente y conspiraron con los elementos conservadores dirigidos por el sobrino de Díaz, Félix Díaz, para fomentar la rebelión.

Consciente de lo pasaba alrededor suyo, Madero llamó a Villa a la capital y le pidió que vigilara el comportamiento de Orozco. Cuando Orozco declaró su intención de derrocar al gobierno de Madero en febrero de 1912, Villa salió inadvertido de la ciudad con 11 seguidores y se dirigió de nuevo a las montañas. Dentro de unos pocos días se unieron a él 500 hombres, la mayoría de ellos antiguos soldados suyos.

Durante varias semanas, Villa llevó a cabo él sólo una campaña contra las fuerzas de Orozco. Después de ganar escaramuzas menores en María del Oro y Guanacevi, envió un aviso claro a las demás guarniciones que contemplaban traicionar al gobierno: Villa

Villa, a caballo, fotografiado durante sus campañas de 1913. Después de la caída del régimen de Díaz en 1911, Villa gozó de un apacible interludio como marido, padre y legítimo hombre de negocios. Al año siguiente, sin embargo, los complots contra el gobierno de su amigo Madero le motivaron a tomar las armas de nuevo.

41

ordenó que todos los prisioneros—tanto los hombres
que hacían el servicio militar obligatorio como los
oficiales—fueran ejecutados. Entonces logró capturar
la ciudad importante de Parral, pero carecía de hombres y municiones para conservarla. Después de una
defensa obstinada de tres días contra una fuerza mayor
que les rodeaba, fue obligado a retirarse.

La situación deterioró tan rápidamente en
México que Madero fue motivado a nombrar a Victoriano Huerta, antiguo general del ejército de Díaz,
para asumir el mando de todas las tropas del gobierno.
El 12 de abril de 1912, Huerta se puso a la cabeza
de las tropas en el norte de México, incluyendo a las
de Villa. El 23 de mayo, mientras que la caballería de
Villa vigilaba los movimientos de la infantería de
Huerta, éste logró desalojar al ejército de Orozco en
la Batalla de Tellano.

La relación entre Villa y Huerta había sido tirante
desde el comienzo: Villa era un hombre orgulloso al
que no le gustaba someterse a las órdenes de nadie, y
Huerta no podía tolerar ni la más mínima forma de
desobedencia. Pero lo que más le molestaba a Villa era
la actitud condescendiente de Huerta. En cuanto
desapareció la amenaza de Orozco, el deterioro de la
relación fue inmediato y dramático.

A pesar o, quizás, a causa de, la importante contribución de Villa a la derrota de Orozco, Huerta
nunca perdía una oportunidad para burlarse de los
modales toscos de Villa, su educación limitada, su
falta de cultura, y su carencia de atuendo militar
apropiado. Villa aguantaba estoicamente el sarcasmo
de Huerta en silencio, pero para apaciguar su orgullo
decidió desobedecer la orden de Huerta contra el
pillaje. Robó de una hacienda varios caballos magnífi-
cos. Tan pronto como Huerta lo supo, ordenó la
detención de Villa.

Al principio, Villa pensó que se trataba nada más
que de un aviso. Pero cuando se le condenó a ser

Victoriano Huerta, antiguo general del ejército de Díaz, fue el comandante de Villa en 1912. Los dos se odiaban, y cuando Villa desobedeció una orden contra el pillaje, Huerta lo mandó detener y lo condenó a muerte.

ejecutado inmediatamente el día después por insubordinación, se dió cuenta de que su vida peligraba de verdad. Incapaz de huir ni de obtener ayuda de sus partidarios, a Villa sólo le quedaba la esperanza de que el Presidente Madero le redujera la pena. Afortunadamente para Villa, el hermano de Madero, Raúl, estaba viajando con el ejército y logró ponerse en contacto con el presidente por telégrafo en el momento justo. De hecho, Villa estaba parado delante del pelotón, esperando la orden para disparar, cuando el telegrama anunciando la suspensión de la ejecución fue entregado al comandante. Para verguenza de Huerta, se le ordenaba trasladar a Villa a la prisión militar en la ciudad de México.

Al llegar Villa a la capital, el Presidente Madero rebajó su condena de la pena capital a dos años de

cárcel. Villa suponía cuando entró en la cárcel menos
rigurosa de Santiago Tlatelolco, que sería soltado dentro de pocos meses. Las condiciones eran muy cómo-
das, tal como convenía a un héroe de la Revolución
Mexicana. Se le permitió pedir las comidas a un
excelente restaurante y de pagar a un joven profesor
que venía diariamente para ayudarle a mejorar a leer y
a escribir. Estudió su libro favorito, *Las campañas de
Napoleón* durante horas y horas, fascinado por la estrategia del general francés del siglo XIX.

Seis meses más tarde, en diciembre, Villa estaba
cansado de esperar el indulto del presidente. Persuadió
a su profesor para que le trajera un sombrero, un chal y
un par de gafas oscuras. Entonces, disfrazado en estos
y otros artículos de ropa que había recogido, se
aprovechó de la vigilancia mínima y un día salió
caminando de la cárcel después de las horas de visita.
Para evitar ser capturado de nuevo en la búsqueda
nacional que se lanzó inmediatamente después, Villa se

*Villa se aleja de un
pelotón el 26 de octubre
de 1912 por la mañana.
Los soldados apuntaban
sus rifles y esperaban la
orden de fuego, cuando llegó
un telegrama anunciando
que el Presidente Madero
había rebajado la pena.*

valió de los trucos que había aprendido cuando era bandido. Tomó varios taxis en direcciones falsas, viajó a Veracruz en dirección al oeste, en vez de al este, y después tomó un barco de Mazatlán a Hermosillo. El último tramo de esta exitosa ruta de huida fue una carrera cruzando la frontera a Nogales, Arizona.

Es muy probable que la fuga de la cárcel y la huida de Villa a los Estados Unidos fueran ayudados por los partidarios de Madero. Varios días antes de escaparse de la cárcel, le visitó un agente de un grupo que buscaba su apoyo para un plan para derrocar a Madero. Tan pronto como llegó a Arizona, Villa le comunicó al Presidente lo que había sabido del complot a través de Abrán González. González, ahora gobernador de Chihuahua, le dió 1,500 pesos a Villa y le aconsejó llevar una vida tranquila.

Villa se mudó a El Paso, Tejas. Con el nombre de Jesús José Martínez, se alojó en un pequeño hotel de dos pisos en la sección mexicana del pueblo, conocido como la Pequeña Chihuahua. A pesar de sus esfuerzos para mantenerse de incógnito, en enero de 1913, algunos periodistas mexicanos y norteamericanos anunciaron su presencia en los Estados Unidos. Varios hasta lograron obtener entrevistas con el reacio fugitivo.

El golpe contra Madero del que había avisado Villa empezó el 9 de febrero de 1913. Ocho días después de empezar la contienda, el General Huerta traicionó a Madero y se apoderó del gobierno. Ambos Madero y su vicepresidente fueron asesinados por su escolta militar pocos días después. Es casi seguro que fue Huerta quien ordenó sus ejecuciones.

El asesinato de Madero desencadenó un espasmo de rebelión social en México por el resto de la década. La autoridad de Huerta para gobernar fue cuestionada casi de inmediato por varios rivales, los más conocidos de los cuales eran Villa, Zapata y Venustiano Carranza,

el gobernador del estado de Cohahuila. El nombre de
Madero se convirtió en un símbolo de la unidad
revolucionaria en la lucha popular vigente en contra
del despotismo militar—representado ahora por el
régimen de Huerta.

Carranza prometió continuar las reformas que
Madero había empezado y se declaró el líder del
movimiento constitucionalista. Villa, dedicado a vengar la muerte de su amigo Madero y eliminar al
odiado Huerta, pidió dinero prestado para comprar
provisiones y salió para la ciudad de Chihuahua con
ocho seguidores.

Incapaz de obtener caballos de forma legal, a causa
de las leyes estadounidenses de neutralidad y la vigilancia de los agentes de Huerta en El Paso, Villa
empleó un truco sencillo pero eficaz. Durante un
poco más de una semana, sus hombres y él alquilaron
caballos de unos establos para dar un paseo a la caída
de la tarde. Cuando una noche no volvieron, el dueño
de los establos se supuso que devolverían los caballos
a la mañana siguiente. Estaba equivocado. Bajo el
amparo de la noche, Villa y sus ocho compañeros
cruzaron a caballo el Río Grande a México.

La creencia de Villa que sus seguidores volverían a
su lado en cuanto regresaba a Chihuahua resultó ser
cierta. Dentro de un mes su ejército había crecido de
ocho hombres a más de 500.

Mientras Villa reunía a sus fuerzas, el comandante
militar de Carranza, Alvaro Obregón, capturó el
pueblo fronterizo de Nogales en Sonora. Los orígenes
humildes de Obregón eran semejantes a los de Villa,
pero este nunca había sido bandido. Aunque no participó en el derrocamiento del régimen de Díaz en la
rebelión de 1910–11, su compromiso a la implemen-
tación de las reformas sociales de la revolución nunca
vaciló. Autodidacta, resultó ser de todos los generales-
ciudadanos mexicanos, el más abierto a las técnicas

Torreón en 1913 cuando Villa hizo de la ciudad el punto central de su campaña contra el gobierno de Huerta. Para poder capturar el importante empalme ferroviario, Villa lanzó una serie de asaltos a los pueblos vecinos, acercándose así a su objetivo principal.

modernas de estrategia y combate militar. Aún así, el liderazgo carismático y la habilidad de reclutar a miles de hombres le permitieron a Villa a eclipsar completamente a Obregón en 1912.

A Carranza y a Villa sólo los unía su oposición común a Huerta. Después de su amarga experiencia de servir bajo Huerta, Villa no estaba a punto de reconocer ningún tipo de órdenes militares superiores. Cuando los emisarios de Carranza se reunieron con Villa en Asunción, Villa dejó claro que era un caudillo—un general a la cabeza de su propio ejército que no tomaba órdenes de nadie. Carranza aceptó con delicadeza las condiciones de Villa y reconoció lo que era obvio al nombrarlo comandante de todas las fuerzas constitucionalistas en Chihuahua. A cambio, Villa reconoció a Carranza como el primer jefe del gobierno constitucionalista revolucionario. Villa se autodesignó General en jefe de la División del Norte.

Villa pasó la mayor parte del verano de 1913 obteniendo de forma clandestina provisiones para su

ejército que crecía. Se les prohibía a los norteamericanos vender material y municiones en México,
pero había contrabandistas dispuestos a proporcionar
casi todo lo que Villa necesitaba con tal de que
pagara en oro los precios exorbitantes que pedían.
De esta manera, Villa pronto tenía a sus fuerzas listas
para la batalla.

    El 25 de agosto de 1913, a la cabeza de 1,200
soldados de caballería, Villa atacó San Andrés, un
pueblo al oeste de la ciudad de Chihuahua. Abrumó a
la guarnición federal de 2,000 hombres y se incautó
de media docena de vagones de ferrocarril atestados
de provisiones y municiones militares. Con esta mina,
pudo equipar a los centenares de reclutas que afluían
a su campamento todos los días.

Los villistas asaltan un emplazamiento federal en noviembre de 1913. Villa se había limitado a las tácticas de asalto rápido que había empleado cuando bandido; en Torreón y Tierra Blanca, se mostró igualmente diestro en el mando de masas de tropas en una batalla formal.

Villa había planeado su campaña con cuidado mientras estaba exiliado en Tejas. Su próxima meta era el importante empalme ferroviario de Torreón. La batalla por la ciudad empezó el 29 de septiembre de 1913. En el curso de los próximos dos días, los villistas atacaron los pueblos vecinos de La Loma, Álvarez, Avilés y Lerdo, a menudo luchando cuerpo a cuerpo; obligaron a los defensores federales a retirarse al perímetro defensivo de Torreón.

Al atardecer del tercer día, los villistas se apoderaron de Torreón en un asalto masivo dirigido por guerrilleros indígenas yaquis. El 1 de octubre, Villa ocupó formalmente la ciudad. Celebró la ocasión fusilando a 50 oficiales federales capturados. Al día siguiente, ordenó a todos los ciudadanos españoles que vivían en la ciudad que abandonaran sus bienes personales y les dio tres horas para que dejaran la ciudad. Incumplimiento de estas órdenes se traduciría en su ejecución inmediata.

El triunfo de Torreón comprobó que Villa era capaz en una batalla convencional de conducir a un ejército grande a la victoria. Las técnicas que había desarrollado cuando era un joven fugitivo en las montañas de Chihuahua contribuyeron de manera inestimable a su éxito anterior como guerrillero. Ahora mostró lo que había aprendido de su estudio en la cárcel de las campañas de Napoleón. El General Francisco Villa ya no era un impulsivo líder de una banda de guerrilleros, sino un administrador, estratega y organizador con unos 10,000 soldados a su cargo.

Las cantidades masivas de aprovisionamiento que obtuvo—cañones, rifles, municiones, un vagón ferroviario blindado, 40 locomotoras, y varios trenes enteros—convirtió a su ejército en una fuerza superior a todas las demás fuerzas revolucionarias de México. El fugitivo había llegado a ser un cazador, el bandido, un general rebelde resuelto a la venganza.

DICTADOR DEL NORTE

*Debidamente vestido
en un riguroso uniforme
militar, Villa era en 1913
el general más poderoso
de México. Como coman-
dante del Ejército del
Norte y dictador de hecho
de Chihuahua, obtuvo
fama internacional—los
oficiales estadounidenses
creían que seguramente
llegaría a ser presidente
de México.*

El poder que los éxitos militares de Villa le confirieron atrajeron la atención de los líderes norteamericanos y europeos en 1913. Por primera vez, su comportamiento después de una batalla fue sometido al escrutinio internacional. La costumbre mexicana que él seguía de ejecutar a todos los oficiales enemigos capturados, le atrajo casi tanta crítica hostil como su maltratamiento de ciudadanos españoles. Muchas de las mujeres y niños españoles que expulsó de Torreón murieron intentando cruzar el desierto; Villa les había prohibido tomar el tren.

Como muchos de sus compatriotas, Villa creía que todos los españoles eran partidarios de Huerta. Había mucho prejuicio popular contra los españoles entre la población mexicana. La mayoría de los mexicanos eran mestizos, gente de herencia mixta española e indígena, y se daban cuenta de que los españoles de pura sangre los despreciaban. Los españoles habían conquistado las antiguas civilizaciones indígenas de México durante el siglo 16, y casi 400 años después, eran los gerentes de las instituciones que más pesaban sobre la gente común: los bancos, las haciendas y las compañías mineras.

Después de expulsar a los españoles, Villa detuvo a 50 alemanes, ingleses, franceses e italianos como re-

henes para evitar un contraataque del gobierno. No se
impuso ninguna restricción al movimiento de
norteamericanos, ya que Villa era demasiado astuto
para provocar una intervención militar por parte de
los Estados Unidos. Cuando descubrió a varios
soldados suyos que no hacían caso de su órden de
saquear sólo la propiedad de los españoles, los fusiló en
el acto. Muchos más fueron fusilados por beber en
exceso o por molestar a civiles inocentes. El mensaje
penetró: Las tropas villistas se comportaban muy bien
para un cuerpo tan dispar de voluntarios.

El próximo objetivo de Villa después de Torreón
fue la ciudad de Chihuahua, que capturó el 8 de
diciembre, después de una retirada estratégica, un arriesgado asalto a Ciudad Juárez y una victoria contundente en Tierra Blanca.

El prejuicio violento de Villa contra los españoles
volvió a salir a la superficie en Chihuahua. Si los 400
residentes españoles de la ciudad no se marchaban en
cinco días, les esperaba el pelotón. Villa mantenía que
tenía que expulsar a todos los ciudadanos españoles al
desierto para evitar su masacre. Aún así, comparado
con su tratamiento de los ricos hacendados que caían
en sus manos, su comportamiento hacia la comunidad
española era en realidad bastante humana.

La audacia, la ingeniosidad y la eficencia de la
campaña villista captaron la imaginación de tanto los
norteamericanos como los mexicanos. Los titulares
que anunciaban sus victorias relampagueaban a través
de la prensa de los Estados Unidos. Los empresarios
con inversiones en México se daban cuenta de la
necesidad de estar del lado que triunfaba. Surgieron
nuevos reclutas y fondos para adquirar provisiones
militares en los Estados Unidos.

Durante el año que Villa ocupó Juárez, pavimentó
las calles, reconstruyó los hospitales, mejoró los ferrocarriles, construyó más escuelas, aumentó los sueldos

de los maestros, cooperó con los oficiales norteamericanos de narcóticos para ayudar a detener el flujo de drogas al otro lado de la frontera y recaudó impuestos de importación y de exportación. Desafortunadamente, también impuso unos impuestos exorbitantes, se incautó de propiedades privadas a voluntad sin recompensar a sus dueños, aplastó disturbios sindicales, permitió el juego y la prostitución y gobernaba por decreto. De hecho, predicaba la democracia, pero practicaba el despotismo.

Para el 1 de enero de 1914, Villa era, a efectos prácticos, el dictador militar del estado de Chihuahua. Nombró un equipo completo de sus propios hombres (seleccionados por su lealtad y no por su capacidad) para llenar todos los puestos gubernamentales. Su influencia, cuando no su control directo, se extendía a lo largo de la mayor parte del norte de México. Todas las fuentes generadoras de ingresos—de la industria,

Un pelotón ejecuta a un trío de prisioneros en el norte de México. Al ser conocido Villa en el mundo entero, sus métodos fueron sometidos al escrutinio internacional. Aunque fue alabado por mejorar las condiciones de vida en Chihuahua, su costumbre habitual de ejecutar a oficiales capturados y de maltratar a europeos atrajo fuertes críticas.

del trabajo y de los impuestos—que estaban a su alcance estaban destinadas al fomento de su pujante máquina de guerra.

La fama de Villa superaba en mucho a la de su jefe nominal, Venustiano Carranza. Para los líderes europeos y el presidente estadounidense, Woodrow Wilson, Villa no era ya uno de los innumerables generales al sur del Río Grande, sino alguien al que se tenía que tomar en cuenta al decidir la política exterior estadounidense con respecto a México. Villa, agudamente consciente del nuevo status que había adquirido, dio muestras de bastante habilidad política. Fomentó el favor de la prensa internacional con la concesión de entrevistas, y tuvo cuidado de tratar a los diplomáticos extranjeros con paciencia y tacto. Hasta autorizó la producción de películas mudas sobre sus hazañas para ser proyectadas en los Estados Unidos. Sus esfuerzos fueron fructíferos. El prestigioso *New York Times,* en un artículo sobre su vida, se refirió a Villa como el Robin Hood de México. El 3 de febrero de 1914, el Presidente Wilson, ansioso de fomentar la caída de Huerta, levantó el embargo que prohibía a los ·comerciantes norteamericanos vender provisiones militares a los insurgentes mexicanos.

El prestigio de Villa a principios de 1914 era tal que la mayoría de los oficiales estadounidenses estaban convencidos de que una vez eliminado Huerta, Villa lo sucedería. El President Wilson despachó a oficiales estadounidenses a México para evaluar la situación. A pesar de que Villa no se había comprometido a ningún programa específico de reforma—aparte del vago deseo de robar de los ricos y dar a los pobres—los informes que recibió Wilson le incitaron a creer que Villa era el individuo adecuado para restaurar el orden en México mientras continuaba las reformas empezadas por Madero. En el tumulto de la guerra civil en México, la persecución por parte de Villa de los ciudadanos españoles fue eclipsado por sus éxitos militares y los puntos débiles de Huerta.

Villa supo los límites de su popularidad en el extranjero durante el llamado asunto Benton. William S. Benton, un ciudadano británico, era dueño de una hacienda extensa en Chihuahua. Incomodado por la continua confiscación de su ganado por los villistas, Benton irrumpió un día a finales de febrero en el cuartel general de Villa y dió expresó sus quejas. Benton y Villa tuvieron una discusión violenta. Al parecer, Benton creía que, como en disputas anteriores con Villa, su calidad de ciudadano británico lo protegería. Estaba equivocado. Villa lo detuvo. Después de un juicio rápido, Benton fue declarado culpable y fusilado.

El destino de Benton no fue diferente al de cualquier mexicano que se atrevía a desafiar la autoridad de Villa, pero la prensa internacional y la comunidad diplomática reaccionaron escandalizadas por el atropello. El hecho de que la muerte de un extranjero le pudiera costar gran parte del favor que había logrado en el extranjero sorprendió de veras a Villa. Aprendió, en esencia, que podía asesinar con tal de no matar a las personas indebidas. Se cuidó mucho de no repetir el mismo error.

Durante la victoriosa campaña militar de la primavera de 1914, Villa mostró que había aprendido bien su lección. Ordenó a su sofisticada unidad médica que cuidara de los prisioneros heridos, y juzgó a los oficiales capturados antes de ejecutarlos. También le dijo al consul norteamericano, Theodore C. Hamm que, debido a que los Estados Unidos había levantado el embargo contra la compra de provisiones militares, no les requeriría a los norteamericanos que enviaban mercancía fuera de México a pagar impuestos de exportación. Dentro de poco, tuvo la oportunidad de

jugar un papel mayor aún en las relaciones entre los Estados Unidos y México.

El 22 de abril de 1914, la infantería de marina de los Estados Unidos desembarcaron en el puerto de Veracruz para castigar al régimen de Huerta por acosar a un grupo de la marina estadounidense. Los marinos llegaron en el momento que un carguero alemán, el *Ypiranga,* estaba a punto de descargar municiones para el ejército federal. Cuando los marinos intentaron parar la entrega, los cadetes de la Escuela Naval Mexicana les dispararon. En la batalla que siguió y que duró dos días, los marinos lograron aplastar toda la resistencia mexicana armada dentro de la ciudad. La invasión de Veracruz provocó una ola de indignación popular a lo largo de México. Una vez más, el matón del norte

El Michigan *(centro) y otros buques de guerra estadounidenses ocupan el puerto de Veracruz en abril de 1914, procurando vengar varios insultos por parte del gobierno de Huerta. En los Estados Unidos, la ocupación fue aclamada como defensa del honor nacional; los mexicanos la condenaron como el gesto de un matón.*

había interferido con la soberanía territorial mexicana. Huerta intentó aprovecharse del furor popular. Invitó a Carranza, a Villa y a Zapata a reunirse con él en una coalición nacional para expulsar a los Yanquis. Se negaron.

Carranza intentó seguir un curso moderado. Aunque la incursión norteamericana le había incomodado personalmente, también era realista. Envió y publicó una carta furiosa de protesta al Presidente Wilson, principalmente para que se difundiera entre los mexicanos; pero no le hizo caso al General Obregón, que aconsejaba combatir, principalmente porque sabía que no podía contar con el apoyo de Villa.

Por varios meses en 1914, la situación en México era muy delicada. México y los Estados Unidos estaban al borde de la guerra. Si Villa se hubiera unido a Huerta, habría comenzado una guerra que los Estados Unidos no quería y que México no se podía permitir. Pero Villa de ninguna manera iba a aliarse con Huerta, especialmente para luchar contra el país del que obtenía todas sus provisiones militares.

Los Estados Unidos se encontraba en la difícil situación de ocupar una ciudad mexicana en medio de una guerra civil, sin el apoyo ni del régimen en el poder, ni de la oposición. Para ayudar a resolver este callejón sin salida, los Estados Unidos animó a Argentina, Brasil y Chile a que se ofrecieran como mediadores. El Presidente Wilson esperaba que algunos diplomáticos latinoamericanos pudieran encontrar alguna manera de combinar la evacuación de Veracruz, la dimisión de Huerta y el establecimiento de un régimen constitucional en México. La llamada conferencia ABC que tuvo lugar en las Cascadas del Niágara en Canadá no logró nada específico pero sí le proporcionó a Carranza una oportunidad para atraer la atención del mundo diplomático internacional. Sin consultar a Villa, despachó a tres delegados para representar al movimiento constitucionalista.

Cuando Villa protestó que Carranza debería haber discutido el asunto con él, Carranza mandó un telegrama a cada uno de los generales de la División del Norte pidiéndoles su apoyo. También les pidió que juraran lealtad a la causa constitucionalista, en lugar de a un individuo en particular. El General Felipe Ángeles, el segundo de Villa, redactó la respuesta de los oficiales de Villa al telegrama de Carranza. Era una declaración afirmando su lealtad a Villa.

El 15 de junio, Villa respondió al esfuerzo de Carranza de socavar su autoridad con su dimisión

Delegados a la Conferencia ABC en las Cascadas del Niágara, Canadá en mayo de 1914. La conferencia no resolvió directamente el conflicto entre los Estados Unidos y México, pero abrió el camino para la dimisión de Huerta.

formal como General en Jefe de la División del Norte. Anunció además que, desde ese día en adelante, obraría independientemente por la pacificación de México y el establecimiento de un gobierno constitucional y de la reforma económica.

Afortunadamente, ambos se dieron cuenta de que el único beneficiario de un conflicto entre ellos sería su enemigo mútuo, Huerta. Prevaleció el sentido común, y Villa y Carranza pudieron negociar un acuerdo el 9 de julio en Torreón, lo que evitó por un tiempo una ruptura total. El acuerdo estipulaba que una convención constitucional tendría lugar en la ciudad de México tan pronto como Huerta fuera derrocado, con el fin de redactar una constitución y crear un gobierno provisional. Los delegados a la Convención, 1 por cada 1,000 soldados en cada uno de los ejércitos revolucionarios, serían elegidos por comités de oficiales de alto rango, sometidos a la aprobación de los comandantes de cada división. Se reestablecería un gobierno civil lo más pronto posible mediante elecciones nacionales abiertas. Se prohibía específicamente a los líderes militares de ocupar el puesto de presidente o de gobernador.

A pesar de la reconciliación aparente, ya no había ni confianza ni respeto entre Carranza y Villa. Públicamente, Carranza ignoró la declaración de independencia de Villa y le ordenó—lo que divirtió a Villa—a seguir adelante con la campaña militar para derrocar a Huerta. Sin embargo, Carranza comenzó en secreto a socavar el poder de Villa interfiriendo con su aprovisionamiento de carbón y municiones. Los trenes de Villa no podían funcionar sin carbón para proporcionar combustible para las locomotoras a vapor. Villa sospechaba que Carranza era el responsable de la escasez de provisiones pero carecía de pruebas, y no le quedaba otro remedio que pasar por alto el asunto hasta que se eliminara a Huerta.

Venustiano Carranza, fotografiado en 1915, después de suceder a Huerta como presidente de México. Carranza y Villa habían tenido varios conflictos cuando ambos eran generales rebeldes, y el nuevo presidente pensaba que no podría gobernar México hasta que tuviera a Villa bajo su control.

Al asegurarse que no habría una guerra entre México y los Estados Unidos, Villa volvió a avanzar hacia el sur. El 23 de junio, su ejército tomó Zacatecas, el último reducto huertista. El 15 de julio, 1914, Huerta dimitió y huyó del país.

Las celebraciones con motivo del derrocamiento de Huerta duraron poco. La tirantez entre Villa y Carranza, contenida mientras atacaban a su enemigo común, afloró. Carranza intentó inmediatamente tomar las riendas del poder, estableciendo un gobierno provisional y declarándose presidente. Villa, convencido de la traición de Carranza, aumentó sus esfuerzos por atraer a reclutas y se retiró con su ejército al norte.

La raíz del problema entre Villa y Carranza era sencilla; cada uno creía que el otro no tenía ninguna intención de implementar reformas y sólo quería convertirse en dictador. Ambos eran, a su manera, líderes revolucionarios atrayentes. Un diplomático estadounidense que conoció a Villa en ese momento le describió como "un hombre muy callado, de maneras corteses; que hablaba en voz baja, pausadamente; intenso, y que a veces se expresaba con emoción, pero siempre discreto, con una corriente de tristeza al fondo." Otro diplomático describió a Carranza como "un hombre de fuerza y no poco talento. Uno de los líderes más capaces de México, y un hombre de rigurosa integridad." La tragedia fue que no había sitio suficiente en el turbulento terreno político de la Revolución Mexicana para que prevalecieran ambos y ellos lo sabían.

AMO DE MÉXICO

Villa y su esposa, María Luz, dan un paseo por las calles de Ciudad Juárez en 1914. Aunque mantenía fielmente a su familia, Villa era un hombre de pasiones incontrolables y su persecución de mujeres era a veces motivó de escándalos embarazosos.

El 15 de agosto de 1914, las fuerzas del General Alvaro Obregón ocuparon la ciudad de México. Cinco días más tarde, Carranza hizo una entrada triunfal en la ciudad y asumió el mando del gobierno. Ningún villista participó en las festividades celebrando la victoria.

La primera confrontación entre las tropas de Carranza y las de Villa ocurrió en Naco, en el estado de Sonora. Debido a que la frontera con los Estados Unidos cruzaba Naco, algunos de los tiros disparados en la sección mexicana hirieron a varios ciudadanos norteamericanos. Este incidente, además de la preocupación de los diplomáticos estadounidenses de que la contienda se extendiera a lo largo de México, motivó un intento de mediación por parte de los Estados Unidos. El Presidente Wilson ansiaba la paz en México y un gobierno democrático estable.

A finales de agosto, los Estados Unidos actuó como mediador en discusiones entre Obregón y Villa. Villa fijó el tono cordial de las negociaciones al saludar a Obregón con el comentario: "Compañero—si usted hubiera venido con tropas, le habríamos recibido con balas, pero como viene sólo, está perfectamente a salvo; Francisco Villa no es traicionero. El destino de nuestro país está en sus manos y en las mías."

Según las condiciones del acuerdo, elaborado trabajosamente entre Villa y Obregón, Villa ordenó a sus tropas a renunciar a su intento de tomar Naco. Por su parte, Obregón prometió que las tropas constitucionalistas no usarían el pueblo como una base para atacar a los villistas. Al concluir las negociaciones, los dos se despidieron, vinculados, al parecer, por una firme amistad. La amenaza de que se prolongara la guerra civil en México parecía haber sido evitada. Una vez más, Villa reconoció a Carranza como su jefe nominal.

El 15 de septiembre de 1914, el Presidente Wilson finalmente ordenó la retirada de las fuerzas estadounidenses de Veracruz. Al parecer, estaba preparado el escenario para la paz en México, salvo por dos problemas: Villa, no Carranza, aún controlaba el ejército más poderoso de México; y Emiliano Zapata, que se había levantado en armas desde el principio de la rebelión contra Díaz, confiaba más en Villa que en Carranza.

La mayoría de los observadores mexicanos y extranjeros supusieron que la disensión entre Villa y Carranza no tardaría en brotar de nuevo, pero la velocidad del estallido les sorprendió. Cuando Obregón volvió a continuar las negociaciones con Villa en Chihuahua, Villa y él discutieron sobre las condiciones exactas de la tregua de Naco. Villa creía que Obregón estaba obligado a ordenar la retirada de la guarnición constitucionalista en Naco puesto que las tropas villistas habían sido trasladadas al sur. Obregón no estaba de acuerdo. Al no estar presente los mediadores estadounidenses, la discusión pronto degeneró en un duelo a gritos. Villa se enfureció tanto que ordenó a sus hombres que rodearan el edificio en que estaban reunidos. Después le informó al exangüe Obregón que su ayudante y él estaban a punto de ser fusilados.

Alvaro Obregón (centro), retratado en 1913, cuando era coronel del ejército constitucionalista. Como general representando al gobierno de Carranza, Obregón negoció con Villa a finales de 1914; al principio progresó, pero cuando Villa finalmente perdió la paciencia, Obregón tuvo que huir porque peligraba su vida.

Aún así, Obregón no cedió. Afortunadamente, algunos ayudantes de Villa pudieron aplacar a su jefe. En lugar de llevar a cabo su mortal amenaza, Villa paró las negociaciones y autorizó a Obregón y a su ayudante a volver en tren a la ciudad de México. A parecer, cambió de opinión después de que Obregón había emprendido su viaje, porque un telegrama fue enviado para detener el tren y tomar a Obregón prisionero en Torreón. Sin embargo, Obregón conocía a Villa lo suficiente para comprender por qué se estaba parando el tren y huyó antes de que los villistas lo pudieran capturar.

El tratamiento de Obregón por Villa motivó a Carranza a parar todo el tráfico ferroviario al norte de Aguascalientes. También ordenó a las fuerzas constitucionalistas que impidieran el avance de los villistas hacia el sur. La respuesta de Villa fue una declaración el 22 de septiembre en que decía que ya no reconocía a Carranza como líder de la revolución porque no había llevado a cabo ninguna de las reformas en que habían convenido en su conferencia en Torreón en julio.

Había una débil esperanza de evitar una nueva guerra civil en México. En las negociaciones en Torreón, Villa y Carranza habían estado de acuerdo de que tuviera lugar una convención nacional en la ciudad de México. Aquí, representantes de todas las facciones revolucionarias elaborarían los detalles para el establecimiento de un nuevo gobierno.

La convención se reunió primero en la ciudad de México a finales de septiembre. Puesto que la capital era la base de Carranza, Villa y Zapata pensaron que controlaría la convención y ambos se mantuvieron alejados. Para aplacarles, los delegados votaron el 5 de octubre a levantar la sesión y reanudarla 10 días más tarde en Aguascalientes. Su estrategia tuvo éxito ya que Villa y Zapata decidieron participar después de todo. Villa se dirigió a los delegados reunidos y, en un discurso emotivo, prometió que ni él ni ninguno de sus generales serían jamás candidatos para presidente ni para gobernador de ningún estado. Prometió apoyar a cualquiera menos a Carranza como presidente provisional. Zapata apoyó la posición de Villa con respecto a Carranza. El 2 de noviembre se logró la selección de un candidato en que ambos lados estaban de acuerdo, el General Eulalio Gutiérrez. Se le ordenó a Carranza que dejara el poder el 10 de noviembre.

El general Emiliano Zapata (sentado en el centro) con miembros de su equipo en 1912. Zapata eran tan poderoso en el sur de México como lo era Villa en el norte; ambos de orígen campesino, los generales rebeldes se admiraban y desconfiaban de los políticos burgueses como Huerta y Carranza.

Carranza denunció la decisión inmediatamente, afirmando que los delegados fueron intimidados por el gran número de tropas villistas dentro y alrededor de Aguascalientes. En lugar de ceder su puesto a Gutiérrez, ordenó a sus generales a volver a sus mandos para prepararse para la batalla. Había empezado una nueva y viciosa fase de la Revolución Mexicana.

El 19 de noviembre de 1914, después de una declaración de guerra formal por parte de Obregón, Villa empezó a avanzar hacia el sur con su poderoso ejército. Tenía 40,000 hombres bien equipados, una reserva de 240 vagones de carbón, de 250 a 300 vagones de provisiones y un amplio número de vagones ferroviarios y locomotoras.

Carranza se dió cuenta de que no tenía ninguna fuerza militar capaz de detener a Villa. Aceptó sagazmente los consejos de Obregón de abandonar la capital y de retirarse a Veracruz. Con las fuerzas mili-

tares de Carranza en retirada, el avance de Villa hacia el sur se transformó de una campaña militar a un desfile triunfal. A diferencia de sus campañas anteriores, Villa ahora se detuvo a sustituir a los oficiales locales con sus propios hombres. Quería asegurarse de que su control político permanente fuera comparable al de su dominio militar.

El 2 de diciembre de 1914, Villa anunció que esperaría a que Zapata se reuniera con él antes de entrar en la ciudad de México para que pudieran compartir la gloria juntos. Cuatro días más tarde, Villa, que llevaba un esmerado traje azul oscuro con aderezos de oro, se juntó con Zapata, quien estaba vestido de campesino con un ancho sombrero. Los dos, cabalgaban a la cabeza de un desfile triunfal de 30,000 hombres a través de las calles de la capital.

Zapata era el adversario más resuelto de todos los régimenes que siguieron a Díaz. Gozaba de una fuerte base de apoyo en su estado natal de Morelos, y había llamado repetidas veces a sus compatriotas a tomar las armas. Como Villa, había presenciado la contínua reducción de tierras comunales durante el régimen de Díaz y consideraba que esta injusticia era el orígen de todos los problemas sociales de México. Puesto que ni Madero, ni Huerta, ni Carranza habían devuelto las tierras a los campesinos tan rápidamente como deberían, según la opinión de Zapata, éste se opuso a cada uno de ellos por las armas.

Contrario a los temores fomentados por Carranza, las tropas de Villa y de Zapata no saquearon ni ejecutaron a miles de ciudadanos. Los comandantes mantuvieron el orden público e impusieron la disciplina militar con firmeza. Las ejecuciones que sí tuvieron lugar ocurrieron discretamente en medio de la noche—tan discretamente, de hecho, que no hay modo de saber exactamente cuántas hubo y cuáles fueron ordenadas por Villa. Contrabalanceando los relatos espeluznantes de ejecuciones a medianoche, había los informes de que Villa recogió a la mayor parte de los huérfanos de guerra de las calles de la capital y los envió a Chihuahua a ser cuidados y educados a expensas suyas.

Aunque Gutiérrez era el presidente provisional de México, Villa y Zapata, los verdaderos centros del poder, prestaban atención a sus órdenes sólo cuando les convenía. Finalmente, la situación se hizo tan intolerable para Gutiérrez que, después de estar en el poder por sólo dos meses, dimitió y huyó al extranjero. La convención en seguida nombró a otro hombre, González Garza, para sustituir a Gutiérrez, pero pronto él también se dió de cuenta que no era nada más que un títere.

En enero de 1915, Villa decidió comenzar la campaña para expulsar a Carranza de Veracruz capturando Tampico e incautándose los yacimientos de carbón de Coahuila. Era una hazaña impresionante controlar la capital, pero hasta que fuera derrotado Obregón y eliminado Carranza, no habría paz en México. El 4 de febrero de 1915, Villa se retiró de la ciudad de México y volvió a su cuartel general en Chihuahua, donde estableció un gobierno provisional y se nombró presidente. Ahora aspiraba claramente a ser el dictador militar de México.

A Villa no le importaba perder la capital; estaba seguro de que la podría recuperar en cuanto eliminara al ejército de Obregón. Para compensar la gran ventaja numérica de Villa, Obregón colocó astutamente a sus hombres en posiciones defensivas cerca del pueblo de Celaya, a aproximadamente 150 millas al noroeste de la ciudad de México.

Obregón seguía las batallas de la Primera Guerra Mundial, que había estallado en Europa en agosto de 1914. Entendía muy bien las ventajas que las trincheras hondas, la artillería masiva y las ametral-

ladoras podían proporcionarle a un ejército. Decidió instalarse en Celaya, porque estaba rodeada de una intricada red de acequias. Obregón ordenó que se vaciaran las acequias de agua y que fueran reforzadas y forradas de alambre de púas. Entonces, colocó a sus tropas y aguardó la ofensiva de Villa.

Después de recibir los informes de vigilancia llevada a cabo de las fortificaciones de Obregón, Felipe Ángeles le aconsejó a Villa de no caer en una trampa. Sería mucho mejor, según mantenían él y otros oficiales, combatir contra Obregón en terreno más apropiado. Villa, exaltado por la serie de triunfos militares, ignoró arrogantemente estos consejos. El 6 de abril lanzó un masivo ataque frontal contra las trincheras de Obregón. Durante más de una semana, en que se repetía la carnicería que tenía lugar en las trincheras de Francia, ola tras ola de la infantería y la caballería villistas eran despedazadas por las ametralladoras y la artillería de campo de Obregón. El tren

Villa cabalga junto a su ejército mientras toma la ofensiva contra el gobierno de Carranza en 1914. En la cumbre de su poder, Villa proyectaba aplastar a las fuerzas en favor de Carranza dirigidas por Obregón y a continuación apoderarse de la ciudad de México.

hospital villista fue abrumado el primer día de la batalla con más de 1,000 bajas. El segundo día de la batalla condujo a los mismos resultados desconsoladores, pero con el doble de bajas.

La pérdida de 3,000 hombres en dos días le obligó a Villa a retirarse. Ángeles, que no estuvo en el lugar de la batalla a causa de la tentativa lograda por parte de una de las divisiones de Obregón de retrasar el avance de su columna, le rogó a Villa que esperara hasta que pudiera reunirse con él antes de lanzar más ataques, pero la llegada de 5,000 refuerzos resultó ser demasiado tentadora para Villa. Decidió volver para atacar de nuevo.

El 13 de abril, al amanecer, grandes nubes de polvo avisaron a Obregón que el ejército villista estaba a punto de iniciar una segunda ofensiva. Obregón estaba listo. Se había aprovechado de la pausa en el combate para mejorar sus fortificaciones. Nuevas minas, más alambre de púas y búnqueres de ametralladoras esperaban a los villistas. La primera táctica de Villa fue repetir el asalto que había fracasado anteriormente; ordenó cargas masivas de la infantería y de la caballería a lo largo de todo el perímetro de Obregón. Los montones de cadáveres de hombres y caballos eran tan altos que las olas posteriores de asaltantes los usaban para taparse hasta que ellos también caían muertos.

Desesperado, con la mitad de sus refuerzos ya casi aniquilados, Villa decidió concentrar a todos sus hombres en una carga a un solo punto determinado del perímetro. Estaba convencido de que el propio peso de su asalto les permitiría triunfar a sus hombres valientes. Estaba equivocado. Obregón, bien preparado para una técnica tal, ordenó que toda su artillería apuntara a la masa expuesta de hombres. La concentración de grandes números de hombres en un solo punto es mortal en la guerra moderna y la carnicería en Celaya fue horrorosa. Miles de villistas fueron pulverizados incluso antes de llegar a la primera línea de defensa. El asalto se convirtió en una retirada y la retirada en una fuga desordenada. La caballería de Obregón completo la masacre; se arrojó sobre los hombres vencidos en un frenesí enloquecido de sablazos.

A la mañana siguiente, Villa, muy consciente de que debido a sus errores de juicio y falta de estrategia adecuada, había perdido la mitad de lo que había sido su orgulloso ejército, aceptó la derrota. A pesar del inmenso número de bajas, pudo retirarse de Celaya de forma ordenada.

Las tropas de Obregón inspeccionan rifles capturados de los villistas en 1915. Al emplear las tácticas militares más avanzadas, Obregón ganó dos victorias decisivas en Celaya y en Aguascalientes, destruyendo así la posibilidad de Villa de gobernar el norte de México.

La derrota en Celaya fue el punto crítico de la carrera militar de Villa. Las cualidades que hasta entonces le habían dado el triunfo—la valentía, la negativa a admitir la derrota, la osadía, la capacidad de liderazgo—eran las características de las que Obregón sacó partido. Después de Celaya, el ímpetu ofensivo se desplazó a Obregón.

Aunque el ejercito villista había sido magullado, no había sido aniquilado. Aún constituía una fuerza de más de 10,000 hombres. Ambos Villa y Obregón sabían que haría falta librar por lo menos otra batalla importante para determinar cuál de los dos ejércitos iba a prevalecer. Villa se preparó para la batalla concentrando sus fuerzas en la zona de Aguascalientes.

Por fin Villa estaba dispuesto a escuchar a Felipe Ángeles, pero era demasiado tarde. A principios de junio, cerca de la ciudad de León en una serie de batallas campales, el dominio genial de Obregón de tácticas modernas de guerra, le permitió derrotar contundentemente a las fuerzas villistas. Obregón perdió el brazo derecho hasta el codo, debido a fuego de artillería, pero se repuso después de una intervención quirúrgica y siguió dirigiendo la batalla.

El ejército de Villa pudo retirarse ordenadamente a Durango desde León; pero, a pesar de ésto, las dos derrotas importantes ocurridas en tan breve espacio destruyeron su reputación como líder invencible. Aumentaron rápidamente las deserciones. Mientras su ejército disminuía, el de Obregón crecía.

Villa todavía controlaba el norte de México durante el verano de 1915, pero fue incapaz de impedir que Obregón derrotara las fuerzas de Zapata y que ocupara la ciudad de México. Para el otoño de 1915 aún faltaba mucho para que se resolviera la situación en México, pero con los triunfos de Obregón el equilibrio del poder se desplazó de nuevo a Carranza.

CAMBIA LA CORRIENTE

Cuando Woodrow Wilson llegó a ser presidente de los Estados Unidos en marzo de 1913, estaba tan horrorizado por la muerte del Presidente Madero a manos del General Huerta que se negó a reconocer el régimen de Huerta. El deseo de ayudar a la desparición de Huerta motivó también la decisión de Wilson de levantar el embargo estadounidense que prohibía abastecer a los mexicanos con provisiones militares.

Después de la derrota de Huerta, Wilson adoptó una política de "espera vigilante," indeciso si apoyar a Villa o a Carranza. Ambos lados reconocieron el gran impacto que tendría el apoyo norteamericano, pero Villa respondió más rápidamente a las instancias diplomáticas que Carranza, y ésto le ayudó a cultivar una opinión favorable en los Estados Unidos.

Desafortunadamente para Villa, su pasado bandolero, su falta de respeto serio por la vida humana, sus numerosas esposas y amantes y su preferencia por las armas para lograr fines políticos proporcionaron a sus enemigos bastantes pretextos en contra de él. Los usaron para mantener una corriente permanente de

Con aspecto confiado, Villa visita a sus tropas durante la campaña contra Carranza. A pesar de sus derrotas en Celaya y en Aguascalientes, Villa seguía convencido de que podía derrocar al gobierno.

propaganda hostil contra Villa en ambos México y los Estados Unidos y socavaron sus esfuerzos para presentarse como un líder revolucionario comprometido.

La tregua que se había negociado entre las fuerzas de Villa y las de Carranza con respecto al pueblo fronterizo de Naco, Sonora, fracasaron en el otoño de 1915. Una vez más los Estados Unidos se involucró directamente porque el combate entre las facciones mexicanas estaba cruzando la frontera. Cuando las protestas norteamericanas no tuvieron resultado, el Presidente Wilson le ordenó al General Hugh L. Scott a mandar un telegrama a Villa en Chihuahua para advertirle que si no se paraba la contienda, intervendrían las tropas de los Estados Unidos.

Villa y el General Hugh L. Scott del Ejército de los Estados Unidos salen de su conferencia en 1915. Según Scott, los dos estuvieron "trabados por dos horas como toros con los cuernos entrecruzados."

Cuando llegó a Naco en octubre de 1915, Villa descubrió que su aliado el Gobernador José María Maytorena había atrincherado a sus tropas delante de las defensas del General Plutarco Calles. Villa, contra las protestas de Maytorena, paró el asedio y ordenó que las tropas volvieran a Agua Prieta. Se llegó a un acuerdo de que Naco permanecería neutral. Ninguno de los lados tenía verdaderamente la intención de cumplir con el acuerdo, pero la retirada mútua convenció al gobierno norteamericano.

A pesar de la cooperación de Villa, Wilson estaba convencido para el otoño de 1915 que Carranza tenía más posibilidad que Villa de establecer un gobierno estable que pudiera mejorar las vidas de la mayoría de los mexicanos. El 15 de octubre de 1915, los Estados Unidos reconoció formalmente al régimen de Carranza como el gobierno de México. El impacto sobre Villa fue inmediato: Wilson prohibió la venta de material y provisiones militares destinadas a Villa, pero autorizó tales ventas al gobierno de Carranza. En la opinión de los Estados Unidos, Villa ya no era un revolucionario, sino alquien que estaba fuera de la ley y el líder de unos bandidos.

Villa recibió la noticia de la decisión de Wilson en Chihuahua mientras reorganizaba su muy disminuido, pero aún poderoso, ejército. Sin duda se sintió traicionado, pero no hizo ninguna declaración pública. Las bajas y las deserciones recientes habían reducido considerablemente el número de tropas bajo su mando, pero aún no estaba vencido. Una victoria importante podría detener su descenso precipitado.

Agua Prieta, al otro lado de la ciudad estadounidense de Douglas, Arizona, era el objetivo lógico de Villa. La guarnición era la única fuerza carrancista del norte de Sonora. Si tomaba Agua Prieta, Villa podía obtener otra entrada fronteriza para pasar provisiones militares de contrabando de los Estados Unidos.

La capacidad de Villa de atacar la guarnición aislada con el peso entero de su ejército renovado de 10,000 hombres parecía garantizar la victoria. El problema era que los gobiernos de Carranza y de los Estados Unidos también se dieron cuenta de que Agua Prieta era el blanco ideal. Esta vez Villa no tendría a su favor el elemento de sorpresa. Cuando su ejército desapareció de vista para llevar a cabo en secreto su largo avance hacia el noroeste, el Presidente Wilson le permitió a Obregón reforzar Agua Prieta transportando tropas de Piedras Negras en la frontera de Tejas con Coahuila a una distancia de 600 millas a través de territorio norteamericano, por líneas ferroviarias estadounidenses.

Al llegar los villistas a Agua Prieta, el pueblo se había convertido en una fortaleza casi impenetrable. Habían llegado vagones de tropas, artillería, municiones y material, y el General Plutarco Calles había rodeado el pueblo de los tres lados con trincheras profundas, montones de alambre de púas, proyectores de luz potentes y centenares de ametralladoras. El cuarto lado daba a territorio norteamericano, así que no necesitaba defensas.

Villa supo de la decisión estadounidense de reconocer formalmente y ayudar al gobierno de Carranza al llegar a los alrededores de Agua Prieta. Le enfureció la nueva política norteamericana. Desde el derrocamiento de Díaz, los Estados Unidos había tenido cuidado de no dar ninguna ayuda material a ninguna facción en México. Nunca se le había permitido a ningún ejército mexicano pisar suelo norteamericano. Ahora, de repente, las reglas habían cambiado. Las fuerzas carrancistas tenían acceso ilimitado a material militar; Villa no tenía ninguno. Las fuerzas carrancistas podían viajar por territorio

Woodrow Wilson, presidente de los Estados Unidos de 1912 a 1920, decidió en el otoño de 1915 que el régimen de Carranza representaba la mayor esperanza para la estabilidad de México. La decisión de Wilson disgustó e incomodó a Villa; le hacía imposible obtener armas y provisiones de compañías norteamericanas.

estadounidense; los villistas no. Villa prometió que tomaría Agua Prieta a pesar de todo.

La batalla de tres días comenzó el 1 de noviembre de 1915 con un duelo de artillería. Villa decidió usar el resto del día para probar las defensas del pueblo con tres cargas de caballería. Mientras que la primera ola de los jinetes villistas cargaron a través de un campo abierto, un viento frío que procedía del desierto agitó una gran nube de polvo que ocultó parcialmente a los asaltantes del fuego enemigo. Sin embargo, el fuego de la artillería y las ametralladoras les obligaron a retirarse a los alrededores del pueblo. Dos cargas más en los otros lados del perímetro defensivo de la ciudad produjeron los mismos resultados descorazonadores. Los pocos que pudieron llegar al pueblo fueron alcanzados pronto por fuego cruzado enemigo.

Los generales de Villa aconsejaron una retirada, pero Villa no estaba dispuesto a aceptarlo. Intentó superar la ventaja defensiva de Calles lanzando su asalto principal bajo la protección de la oscuridad. Antes de la señal para atacar a la 1:30, las tropas villistas yaquis habían avanzado cautelosamente en silencio por una línea de alambre de púas, en preparación para tirar granadas dentro de las fortificaciones enemigas. Era un buen plan, pero carecía del elemento de sorpresa porque Calles había anticipado la estrategia y había preparado su propia sorpresa. Al empezar los Yaquis su asalto, los hombres de Calles encendieron enormes proyectores de luz eléctricos, convirtiendo la noche en día. Los Yaquis habían caído en una trampa. No podían avanzar en la luz cegadora y el alambre de púas estaba a sus espaldas. Sólo podían permanecer donde estaban y ser asesinados. Los compañeros que se precipitaron en su ayuda sufrieron la misma suerte.

No se supo la magnitud de la catástrofe hasta la mañana siguiente cuando se pudieron ver miles de cadáveres que cubrían el campo de batalla. La combinación de proyectores de luz y ametralladoras añadían un nuevo elemento a la lucha entre Villa y Carranza. No había ninguna duda para Villa que las luces y la electricidad y los conocimientos necesarios para hacerlos funcionar habían sido proporcionados por los Estados Unidos.

Las victorias anteriores de Villa habían atraído a reclutas que afluían a su bandera; con sus derrotas su ejército disminuía. Para facilitarles la recogida de alimentos a sus tropas, dividió los retazos de su ejército en tres grupos. A cada grupo se le ordenó forrajear por caminos diferentes hasta llegar a Hermosillo, donde el ejército se volvería a reunir. Pero sólo el grupo bajo el mando personal de Villa llegó a Hermosillo. Los otros dos simplemente se dispersaron por el camino.

Como expresión de su resentimiento contra los Estados Unidos, Villa exigió que todas las compañías mineras en su zona le dieran un préstamo de $25,000; sino, serían confiscadas. Ahora sus hombres y él consideraban como suya toda propiedad norteamericana que estuviera a su alcance.

Villa se dió cuenta de que le faltaba tiempo. Cuanto más esperaba, más apoyo recibían sus enemigos de los Estados Unidos. Sabía que su ejército apaleado aún era capaz de una gran ofensiva más y decidió atacar Hermosillo. Puesto que ya no tenía fondos para pagar a sus hombres, Villa les prometió permitirles saquear la ciudad.

La batalla de Hermosillo a mediados de noviembre de 1915 fue una derrota menos dramática pero aún más contundente que la de Agua Prieta. Una vez más la valentía y la disciplina de las tropas villistas cedieron ante el fuego de artillería y el agotador fuego cruzado de las ametralladoras. Ni se les dignó con una retirada ordenada; equipados ahora con artillería de larga distancia, los carrancistas siguieron disparando a los villistas, convirtiendo su retirada en una fuga aterrada y desordenada. La carnicería facilitada por la ayuda estadounidense e infligida por los carrancistas acabó en esencia con el ejército de Villa. Nunca más podría representar una importante amenaza militar al gobierno de Carranza.

Mientras que los retazos del ejército villista en proceso de desintegración volvían en grupos revoltosos hacia el norte a Nogales, cometieron varias atrocidades. Villa era impotente a controlar a sus hombres. Puede que hasta los animara. Hubo personas que dieron testimonio que puesto que las municiones escaseaban, mataba a prisioneros colocándolos en fila uno tras otro; encañonaba el pecho del primero y disparaba. Entonces, determinaba cuántos habían

El presidente mexicano Carranza posa con sus nuevos reclutas en 1915. Reforzado por el nuevo material de los Estados Unidos, incluyendo las ametralladoras más modernas, los carrancistas infligieron otras dos derrotas aplastantes a Villa en Agua Prieta y Hermosillo.

muerto, los apartaba y volvía a colocar en fila a los sobrevivientes y repetía el proceso.

Cuando los soldados alcanzaron la comunidad fronteriza de Nogales, su rabia contra los Estados Unidos por interferir en los asuntos internos de México se desbordó. El 25 de noviembre, varios soldados, blandiendo armas, cruzaron a caballo la frontera internacional y amenazaron a dos oficiales estadounidenses. Anticipando más problemas, el comandante militar regional pronto reforzó la guarnición local con más hombres y autorizó a sus tropas a devolver fuego enemigo. Fuego del lado mexicano de la frontera provocó varios tiroteos intensos antes de que las fuerzas carrancistas que venían persiguiendo a los villistas, entraron finalmente en Nogales el 26 de noviembre.

El mismo patrón de comportamiento belicoso y tiroteos que llegaban al otro lado la frontera se repitió en Ciudad Juárez hasta que las fuerzas carrancistas tomaron posesión de esa ciudad el 23 de diciembre de 1915. Con la toma de Ciudad Juárez, la derrota de Villa en el norte de México parecía concluida hasta tal punto que los diplomáticos norteamericanos auguraron confiadamente que pronto se fugaría a los Estados Unidos.

En lugar de pedir asilo político al otro lado de la frontera, Villa volvió a la ciudad de Chihuahua. Ahí en una reunión tumultuosa, sus generales le informaron que ya no debía contar con su apoyo. La nueva política norteamericana de apoyar a Carranza parecía haber logrado su meta. Villa ya no parecía presentar una amenaza seria a la estabilidad del gobierno. Con una pequeña banda de sus secuaces más leales, Villa desapareció en el terreno escarpado de la Sierra Madre. Pero no había dejado de ser noticia.

COLUMBUS

En enero de 1916, los fragmentos de la diezmada División del Norte empezaron a regruparse en las montañas de Chihuahua. El 10 de enero, Pablo López uno de los oficiales villistas, dirigió una emboscada que logró capturar un tren cerca de Santa Ysabel. Después de robar a los pasajeros mexicanos en el primer vagón, López siguió al segundo y descubrió que un grupo de directores de minas norteamericanos estaban a bordo con rumbo a la ciudad de Chihuahua. Gritando "¡Viva Villa!" López y sus hombres empezaron a disparar a los norteamericanos desarmados mientras estaban sentados o mientras intentaban huir al desierto. Murieron diecisiete. El único sobreviviente de la masacre, que pudo escapar porque se escondió en la maleza mientras eran asesinados sus colegas, les proporcionó testimonio escalofriante del incidente a la prensa norteamericana y mexicana.

Villa admitió que ordenó el ataque al tren, pero negó haber autorizado a López a herir ciudadanos norteamericanos. Es posible, si se considera la situación en que se encontraba Villa en ese momento, que de hecho autorizó el asalto y la masacre para desestabilizar las nuevas relaciones armoniosas entre el gobierno de Carranza y los Estados Unidos. Si así fue, la maniobra casi tuvo éxito. En el Congreso de los Estados Unidos se pedía intervenir en México. Pero el

Después de su asalto a Columbus, Nuevo México, en 1916, Villa fue una figura odiada en los Estados Unidos. Aquí lo ahorcan en efigie en el desfile anual de los Mummers en Filadelfia.

gobierno de Carranza se esforzó por capturar a los culpables y los Estados Unidos se estaban envolviendo en la Primera Guerra Mundial. Prevalecieron los elementos políticos moderados en el Congreso. Varios meses después, los carrancistas capturaron a López y lo condenaron a muerte. Poco antes de ser ejecutado, sostuvo que Villa había ordenado la masacre de Santa Ysabel.

Santa Ysabel fue un momento crítico en las relaciones estadounidenses con Pancho Villa. Ya no hubo en la prensa más referencias a Pancho Villa como un moderno Robin Hood mexicano. El incidente eliminó toda posibilidad de Villa de obtener asilo político. En cuanto a Villa, los sentimientos positivos que había tenido hacia los Estados Unidos se trocaron en amargura al ser considerado el responsable de las acciones de un oficial enfurecido que estaba sólo nominalmente bajo sus órdenes.

La desintegración de su ejército, junto con la notoriedad de la masacre de Santa Ysabel, motivó a Villa a adoptar medidas desesperadas. Durante la primera semana de marzo, dirigió a los 500 hombres que aún le seguían al pueblo fronterizo de Las Palomas, Chihuahua, situado a pocas millas de Columbus, Nuevo México. El comandante de la guarnición militar norteamericana recibió varios informes diciendo que Villa proyectaba cruzar la frontera para atacar a Columbus, pero ya que la información era insuficiente y había otros informes contradictorios, no puso en estado de alarma a su guarnición de 300 hombres.

El 8 de marzo, varios periódicos en El Paso, Tejas, informaron que Villa, acampado cerca de Las Palomas, había ordenado la ejecución de dos prisioneros norteamericanos. El General John J. "Black Jack" Pershing, el comandante de las fuerzas estadounidenses en Fort Bliss recibió esta noticia y la del supuesto plan de ataque a Columbus. También había información contradictoria que situaba a Villa en otro lugar, a punto de atacar a la guarnición carrancista en Las Palomas. Pershing no sabía cuál de los informes creer. De todas formas, podía hacer muy poco. Si quería reforzar Columbus, tenía que debilitar seriamente a otras guarniciones que podían ser objetivos de Villa. Puesto que Villa estaba avanzando por el lado mexicano de la frontera no había manera en que Pershing podía obtener información fidedigna y regular sobre su situación e intenciones.

Villa pronto despejó todas las dudas. A las 4 de mañana, el martes, 9 de marzo de 1916, sus hombres se abalanzaron sobre Columbus bajo el amparo de la oscuridad disparando a todas partes y arrojando antorchas a edificios. Gritos de "¡Viva Villa!" "¡Viva México!" "¡Muerte a los Americanos!" y los gemidos de los hombres heridos estallaron el silencio de la madrugada. Al cabo de poco tiempo, el pueblo indefenso estaba en llamas, y ocho civiles norteamericanos yacían moribundos, acribillados a balazos.

Tropas del 13 regimento de Caballería de los Estados Unidos observan el cadáver de un asaltante mexicano después del ataque de Villa a Columbus. El atrevido asalto de madrugada pudo haber triunfado si no fuera por el valor de unos pocos soldados estadounidenses que mantuvieron a raya a los asaltantes hasta que el resto de la guarnición estaba despierta.

La forma tan metódica de proceder de los villistas por los edificios y las calles de Columbus hacía pensar que habían explorado la ciudad antes del asalto. Sabían dónde protegerse de las ametralladoras de la guarnición y pronto encontraron a las personas que tenían acceso a dinero y a mercancías. El cuidado con que mataban sólo a hombres mostraba que los secuaces de Villa actuaban según órdenes precisas.

Arthur Ravel de 16 años sobrevivió y pudo contar lo que fue estar esa mañana en Columbus: "Estábamos en el edificio del Hotel Comercial, y ví a la Sra. Ritchie—creo que era ella—en el bar del Sr. Walker, rogándoles a los mExicanos que no mataran al Sr. Ritchie. Le oí a uno de los mexicanos decir: 'Si ves a un blanco, mátalo.' " Después de presenciar la muerte de otros hombres esa mañana, a Ravel se le perdonó la vida para que pudiera abrir la tienda de su padre. Su descripción de lo que ocurría mientras caminaba acompañado por dos villistas es muy gráfica. "Volaban balas en todas direcciones; había incendios en todas partes; de vez en cuando veías a un hombre que caía muerto. Los ví saquear nuestra tienda y la tienda del Sr. Walker, una ferretería; se llevaban sillas de montar, herramientas y otras cosas." Ravel se salvó sólo porque los dos mexicanos que le servían de escolta fueron asesinados por los del pueblo.

El asalto tan cuidadosamente preparado por Villa pudo haberle permitido capturar Columbus si no fuera por la disciplina y el valor que mostraron las tropas norteamericanas. Al empezar el ataque, sólo estaban despiertos unos pocos guardias y un grupo de cocineros negros que estaban preparando el desayuno. Los cocineros no tenían rifles cargados; las armas y las municiones se guardaban bajo llave en la armería. Pero cuando empezaron los tiros, los cocineros no huyeron aterrados. Se defendieron con las únicas armas que tenían a mano—agua hirviente, cuchillos de cocina, ollas y sartenes. Su valor y el de los soldados que peleaban con porras y con las propias manos le ganó el tiempo suficiente a la guarnición. Al cabo de poco tiempo, el resto de los soldados estaban despiertos y bien armados.

El contraataque lanzado por las tropas norteamericanas le obligó a Villa a llamar de nuevo a sus hombres al amanecer. Aunque el asalto duró poco más de una hora, fueron masivos los estragos físicos y psicológicos causados por el pillaje y el combate en las calles llenas de humo de Columbus. Muchos residentes, temiendo otro asalto y más atrocidades, empezaron a huir a pie de la zona.

Villa dejó un pequeño destacamento para cubrir su retirada y cabalgó hacia el sur de vuelta a México. Los soldados enfurecidos no estaban dispuestos a permitir que los villistas se escaparan tan fácilmente. Una columna de 60 soldados de la caballería norteamericana subyugaron a la retaguardia y entraron en México, persiguiendo a los villistas por ocho horas. Hubo varias escaramuzas antes de que la falta de municiones y el agotamiento les obligó a volver a Columbus.

Los villistas pagaron un precio muy alto por la audacia de su líder—murieron 167, fueron capturados 13 y muchos más fueron heridos. Nunca se sabrá exactamente por qué Villa decidió atacar Columbus, pero existen varias posibilidades: una represalia contra la ayuda estadounidense a Carranza; la necesidad de provisiones que faltaban; el deseo de castigar a un comerciante que no había entregado municiones ya adquiridas; y la creación de una disputa entre el gobierno estadounidense y el de Carranza sobre la necesidad de intervención norteamericana.

Desde un punto de vista militar, el asalto de Villa fue un desastre: las bajas eran casi la mitad de sus hombres. Sin embargo, desde una perspectiva política fue un éxito total. La respuesta de los Estados Unidos humilló a Carranza y restauró el prestigio de Villa entre la población mexicana.

Carranza se negó a autorizar la intervención norteamericana; a pesar de ésto, el día después del asalto, el Presidente Wilson ordenó al ejército de los Estados Unidos a vengarse. El General Pershing organizó un cuerpo que estaba decidido a perseguir a los villistas al interior de México si fuera necesario, para capturarlos o destruir su capacidad de causar más problemas a lo largo de la frontera.

La Expedición Punitiva de 3,000 hombres entró en México el 15 de marzo de 1916, en dos columnas distintas: una desde Columbus y la otra desde Culberson's Ranch, situado en el suroeste de Nuevo México. Pershing ordenó a la caballería de Culberson que alcanzara a Colonia Dublán, una comunidad de mormones norteamericanos, en dos días. Esperaba que la columna llegara a tiempo para proteger a la gente que vivía ahí de la furia de Villa, al mismo tiempo que impedía la huída de Villa hacia el sur. La columna de Culberson logró la primera meta, pero no pudo interceptar la retirada de Villa.

El segundo destacamiento de las fuerzas de Pershing llegó a Colonia Dublán tres días más tarde, el

El General John J. "Black Jack" Pershing, comandante de las fuerzas norteamericanas en Fort Bliss, Tejas, dirigió la incursión de 3,000 tropas en México para perseguir a Villa en marzo de 1916. Así el asalto de Columbus logró el objetivo principal de Villa—distanciar a los Estados Unidos del régimen de Carranza, que se opuso resueltamente a la invasión de Pershing.

Miembros de la Compañía E del 24 Regimento de la Infantería de los Estados Unidos ocupan las trincheras en Colonia Dublán, México, en julio de 1916. Las tropas alcanzaron la ciudad a tiempo para proteger a los residentes que eran ciudadanos estadounidenses de la furia de Villa, pero llegaron demasiado tarde para impedir la fuga del líder bandolero a las montañas.

20 de marzo. Al día siguiente, la expedición reunida penetró en México. Empezó el largo proceso de localizar a los grupos dispersados de villistas.

Villa utilizó los seis días entre el asalto a Columbus y la llegada de la columna Culberson para desaparecer en el salvaje y montañoso terreno de Chihuahua que conocía tan bien. Sus perseguidores, aún con la ayuda de guías Apache, nunca lo pudieron atrapar, a pesar de que fue visto en varias ocasiones y de que una vez fue herido por un disparo debajo de la rodilla izquierda. Debido a su habilidad de escabullirse contínuamente durante 11 meses mientras lo buscaban las pequeñas y rápidas patrullas de la Expedición Punitiva, Villa se convirtió en un héroe popular nacional.

La indignación de la población mexicana ante la presencia de las tropas de Pershing en suelo nacional le presentaba a Carranza un dilema imposible. Aunque quería que Villa fuera capturado, las necesidades políticas le obligaron a dificultar al máximo la tarea de la Expedición Punitiva. Cuánto más tiempo permanecían las tropas en México y cuánto más al sur descendían, más crecía el enfado de la población.

Después de enfrentarse las fuerzas de Pershing con tropas mexicanas en dos ocasiones distintas, el Presidente Wilson fue obligado a movilizar la Guardia Nacional estadounidense a lo largo de la frontera para evitar asaltos.

Si se tienen en cuenta las dificultades que tuvo la expedición: la necesidad de aprovisionar a 3,000 hombres en el áspero y salvaje terreno de la Sierra Madre, la falta de cooperación por parte del gobierno de Carranza, la astucia de Villa, y la creciente animosidad del público mexicano, Pershing manejó hábilmente la situación. Nunca capturó a Villa, pero logró perseguirlo por más de un año al mismo tiempo que evitaba una guerra de gran envergadura con México.

El 1 de septiembre de 1916, Villa desafió a Pershing y resumió sus actividades guerrilleras con un ataque victorioso a una fuerza militar carrancista cerca de Satevo. Tres semanas más tarde, dirigió un asalto en la ciudad de Chihuahua; obtuvo una gran cantidad de municiones y liberó a 1,600 prisioneros de la cárcel. La mayoría de ellos se unieron a su banda. El 23 de noviembre, después de tres días de combate encarnizado, los villistas expulsaron a la guarnición carrancista de la ciudad de Chihuahua.

Cuando Villa ocupó Chihuahua el 23 de noviembre, no intentó refrenar el comportamiento de sus hombres. Ocurrieron múltiples atrocidades; la más notoria fue el robo sistemático y la masacre en sangre fría de la población china de la ciudad. Como la mayoría de los campesinos mexicanos, Villa odiaba a los chinos que habían inmigrado a México. Su aspecto físico y sus costumbres diferentes, su establecimiento de pequeñas empresas, y los rumores de que escondían todo su dinero en la ropa les convertían en objetivos tentadores para los atropellados campesinos mexicanos. Al espiar a sus víctimas chinas, los villistas les disparaban para que fuera más fácil registrarles en busca de su dinero.

Tropas estadounidenses ocupan uno de los vehículos armados empleados por la Expedición Punitiva. Los conocimientos que tenía Villa del escarpado terreno de la Sierra Madre le permitieron eludir a sus perseguidores por casi un año, una hazaña que añadió a su leyenda como héroe popular mexicano.

Para enero de 1917 era obvio que la Expedición Punitiva carecía de hombres para eliminar a Villa como factor en los asuntos mexicanos. Pershing declaró que la única manera en que podía lograr su meta era reforzar a su ejército y ocupar el norte de México. Sabía que los Estados Unidos no estaba preparado para una intervención masiva. Las prioridades del país se habían desplazado de México a Europa. En lugar de empezar una guerra con México en vísperas del envolucramiento de los Estados Unidos en la Primera Guerra Mundial, el Presidente Wilson le ordenó a Pershing a retirar sus fuerzas.

Cuando las últimas tropas estadounidenses cruzaron la frontera el 5 de febrero de 1917, la responsabilidad de mantener el orden en el norte de México cayó una vez más en los soldados del gobierno de Carranza. Tanto Carranza como Villa agradecieron la oportunidad de enfrentarse de nuevo.

LA ÚLTIMA CAMPAÑA

Villa, durante los últimos años de su carrera militar, mientras luchaba por mantener a su ejército y su prestigio como comandante. Aunque lanzó varios asaltos victoriosos entre 1917 y 1918, la fuerza combinada del gobierno de Carranza y el de los Estados Unidos finalmente le obligó a retirarse.

En abril de 1917, poco después de que los Estados Unidos declaró la guerra contra Alemania, Villa reanudó sus ataques a las guarniciones carrancistas cerca de la frontera estadounidense. El 30 de mayo, los villistas obligaron a la guarnición en Ojinaga a refugiarse en el lado norteamericano de la fontera. Sin embargo, esta vez Villa no hizo ningún esfuerzo para reforzar y guardar el pueblo. Tres días después de capturar Ojinaga, desapareció con sus hombres a las montañas donde pasaría el verano. La guarnición de Ojinaga pronto volvió y ocupó el pueblo de nuevo, pero fue expulsado otra vez por Villa al otro lado de la frontera el 15 de noviembre.

A lo largo de 1918, Villa continuó a reconstruir su ejército mientras dirigía una serie de asaltos contra guarniciones carrancistas aisladas. En cuanto se terminó la cosecha del otoño, atacó y saqueó Villa Ahumada, en la línea de ferrocarril Juárez-Chihuahua. El 12 de diciembre, asaltó la comunidad minera en Cusihuiriachic y se incautó de $10,000 de la caja fuerte de la compañía. También quemó el depósito de leña de la compañía. Según él, esto era para obligar a la compañía a comprar más leña y así crear más trabajos para la gente. Un asalto similar ocurrió el 22 de enero de 1919 contra otra compañía minera en Santa Eulalia.

En cuanto crecieron de nuevo su ejército y su prestigio, el comportamiento de Villa cambió. Volvió a comportarse más bien como un líder guerrillero revolucionario que un bandido. Durante los asaltos, dedicaba tiempo a echar discursos, animando a la gente a luchar por sus derechos, y se cuidó de no herir a ningún norteamericano o extranjero. Una vez más, se podía preocupar de su fama internacional.

Para la primavera de 1919, Villa dirigía un ejército bien equipado y bien entrenado de más de 1,500 hombres. El 19 de abril de 1919, después de una corta batalla, Villa volvió a capturar Parral. Para evitar publicidad negativa, cerró la ciudad a periodistas mientras sus hombres saquearon más de un millón de dólares en oro de las cajas fuertes de varias compañías. No se tocaron los bienes de los extranjeros, pero los edificios mexicanos fueron robados. Antes de partir, Villa supervisó personalmente las ejecuciones de prisioneros que le habían abandonado para apoyar a Carranza.

El oro robado de Parral le permitió a Villa pagar a sus hombres, equipar nuevos reclutas y adquirir armas modernas y municiones que le hacían mucha falta. Su próxima meta en su bien planeada vuelta al poder fue obtener su antigua base de operaciones cerca de la frontera, Ciudad Juárez.

Un poco después de la medianoche del 14-15 de junio, Villa lanzó uno de sus clásicos ataques nocturnos contra la guarnición de Ciudad Juárez. A las 2 de la madrugada, los villistas lograron explusar las tropas carrancistas a la Fortaleza Hidalgo. Parecía que la batalla estaba ganada, pero entonces, poco antes del amanecer las tropas carrancistas contra-atacaron y volvieron a capturar una parte considerable de la ciudad.

Después de una pausa matinal, el combate se reanudó. En cuanto volvió a oscurecer, Villa ordenó a sus hombres a tomar la ofensiva. El combate se hizo

Encabezados por un vehículo blindado, las tropas estadounidenses del 24 Regimiento de Caballería ocupan una sección de Ciudad Juárez, México, en junio de 1919. Un asalto masivo por parte de unidades de la artillería, la infantería y la caballería de los Estados Unidos el 15 de junio, aniquiló el ejército de Villa y le eliminó como factor en la política mexicana.

tan intenso que varias balas de ambos lados empezaron a volar con bastante frecuencia al otro lado de la frontera con los Estados Unidos. A aproximadamente las 11 de la noche, después de que tres soldados y varias mujeres habían sido asesinados por balas dispersas, el comandante norteamericano en Ciudad Juárez envió un mensaje brusco a los carrancistas—"Quitense de en medio si no quieren ser heridos"—y ordenó a sus hombres a entrar en la refriega contra Villa.

Un mortal fuego de artillería anunció la decisión norteamericana. Centenares de proyectiles explosivos llovieron sobre las tropas de Villa en el hipódromo de Ciudad Juárez y a través de la ciudad, mientras los soldados negros de la infantería norteamericana avanzaban en masa al otro lado del puente internacional con las bayonetas armadas. Y a la vez, dos columnas de la Séptima Caballería cruzaron el Río Grande en un puente flotador para impedir la huida de los villistas al desierto. La derrota era completa. Al amanecer, el ejército que Villa había nutrido

cuidadosamente por más de dos años había sido aniquilado.

Villa apenas escapó la carnicería en Ciudad Juárez. Logró evitar ser capturado cambiándose frecuentemente de lugar y viajando con unos pocos secuaces leales hasta alcanzar su antiguo escondite de bandido en las montañas de Chihuahua. Su antiguo aliado, Emiliano Zapata, no fue tan afortunado. Fue traicionado por uno de sus propios oficiales por la recompensa ofrecida por Carranza y fue asesinado por una bala de asesino. A finales de 1919, Villa sabía que le esperaba el mismo destino que Zapata, pero juró que nunca se rendiría mientras Carranza era presidente.

Villa no tuvo que esperar mucho tiempo. Después de que Carranza llegó a ser presidente constitucional en mayo de 1917, no hizo mucho para implementar tales reformas fundamentales como: la distribución de tierras, el control de los recursos naturales y la legislación social y sindical que prometía la radical constitución de 1917. A principios de 1920, cuando Carranza intentó imponer la elección de su candidato para sucesor, cerró su suerte. Alvaro Obregón, el brillante estratega militar que le había llevado al poder, volvió de su retiro para asegurar su desaparición. Carranza esperó demasiado para intentar escapar. Entorpecido por los sacos de oro que había intentado robar del tesoro, fue capturado y asesinado en las montañas en camino a Veracruz el 21 de mayo de 1920.

Obregón resultó ser un sincero y elocuente campeón de los principios fundamentales de la Revolución Mexicana según se expresan en la Constitución de 1917. La elección de Obregón como presidente el 1 de diciembre de 1920, después de unos meses de gobierno interino bajo Adolfo de la Huerta, señaló el comienzo de la vuelta al orden interno en México después de una década de sangriento caos social y político.

Alvaro Obregón, que había perdido el brazo derecho mientras derrotaba a Villa en la Batalla de Aguascalientes en 1915, llegó a ser presidente de México en 1920. Uno de los mejores líderes mexicanos, Obregón era capaz de tratar a los antiguos enemigos con gran generosidad: le permitió a Villa retener sus privilegios militares y le concedió una propiedad muy grande.

Con la desaparición de Carranza, Villa aceptó la necesidad de aceptar la derrota. Las condiciones que le ofrecía su antiguo enemigo eran extremadamente generosas: se le permitía a Villa retener el rango de general a sueldo completo, y como recompensa por sus anteriores servicios a la revolución se le concedió el magnífico Rancho del Canutillo de 25,000 acres.

Jubilado a la edad de 43 años, Villa se entregó por completo al mejoramiento de la productividad de su nueva propiedad y la modernización de la ciudad cercana de Parral, dando muestras de la misma energía que había empleado para formar su famosa División del Norte. La generosa pensión que recibía y las ganancias de la cuidadosa gerencia de su hacienda le permitieron adquirir maquinaria y los talentos de expertos agrícolas.

En sus relaciones con su familia y sus obreros, Villa representaba el estereotipo de comandante militar jubilado y déspota ilustrado. Volvió a vivir con su mujer legítima, María Luz y envió a sus dos hijos menores a un colegio privado en Tejas. Para los hijos de sus obreros, hizo construir una escuela en la hacienda y trajo a un maestro.

Villa parecía gozar de veras de su nueva vida tranquila y aparentemente no quería mal a nadie. Agasajó a numerosos mexicanos, europeos y norteamericanos en su hacienda. Una vez, en un encuentro fortuito con un norteamericano en un viaje en tren, le permitió manejar sus famosos revólveres con mango de nácar y hasta le mostró las cicatrices en la pierna izquierda donde le habían herido los soldados de Pershing.

La vida de familia en Canutillo era agradable pero insegura. Había demasiadas personas en México cuyos parientes habían muerto a causa de Pancho Villa y había mucha gente en puestos importante que temían que no se mantuviera jubilado. Mientras vivía Villa, permanecía la amenaza de disturbios internos en México. Al cabo de poco tiempo, los enemigos de Villa reunieron unos $50,000 por su asesinato.

Villa, fascinado siempre por los automóviles, solía salir a pasear en un sedán Dodge. El viernes, 20 de julio de 1923, mientras volvía a casa de Parral con sus guardaespaldas, Villa observó a un vendedor ambulante que le saludaba en un cruce. Redujo la velocidad para devolverle el saludo, y el vendedor gritó "¡Viva Villa!" El grito era la señal para una unidad de asesinos pagados escondidos en una casa al lado de la carretera. Los asesinos apuntaron los rifles y

Villa y uno de sus guardaespaldas, el Coronel Trillo, yacen muertos en el sedán Dodge de Villa después de un emboscada el 20 de julio de 1923. Jesús Salas Barrazas, un congresista que participó en el asesinato, fue condenado a 20 años de cárcel por el delito, pero cumplió sólo seis meses de la condena.

dispararon sobre el Dodge que viró bruscamente y se estrelló contra un árbol. Villa murió instantáneamente, acribillado por siete balas. Cuatro de sus guardaespaldas murieron con él.

Varios meses después, Jesús Salas Barrazas, el congresista para el distrito El Oro de Durango y un partidario de Obregón, a quien Villa había golpeado en una ocasión con una pistola por un asunto de faldas, fue detenido y acusado del asesinato. Se declaró inocente pero fue condenado a 20 años de cárcel. En realidad sólo cumplió seis meses de la condena. Poco antes de morir en 1951 en la ciudad de México, Barrazas confesó que había sido uno de los siete hombres que habían emboscado a Villa.

Villa fue enterrado en el cementerio de Parral, pero ni en la muerte le dejaron en paz. La tumba fue profanada por ladrones en 1926; se llevaron la cabeza la cual nunca fue recuperada.

Al repasar la vida de Villa es difícil a menudo separar los hechos de la leyenda. Para sus críticos, la carrera de Villa como bandido antes de la revolución es una prueba de que era culpable de todos los delitos que se le atribuyen. Los críticos creen que no era otra cosa sino un asesino patalógico cuyo compromiso profesado para con la revolución era sólo un pretexto para asesinar. Para sus partidarios, Villa era el epítome del campesino rebelde, un hombre que carecía de cultura pero que poseía ideales e inteligencia. Según los admiradores de Villa, mataba para sobreivir, pero siempre se mantuvo fiel a su compromiso a distribuir la riqueza nacional.

El pueblo del norte de México buscó y encontró en Pancho Villa un salvador que infligía venganza a los hacendados y los dueños de las minas que ellos no podían alcanzar. Villa era un héroe para ellos porque muchas de sus extraordinarias hazañas, tanto generosas como viciosas, eran típicas de sus orígenes

Acribillado a balazos, el cadáver de Villa yace en el hospital en Parral, esperando una autopsia. Los historiadores siguen debatiendo el lugar de Villa en la historia de México, pero para el pueblo del norte de México, él sigue siendo un héroe popular que luchó por los derechos de los desvalidos.

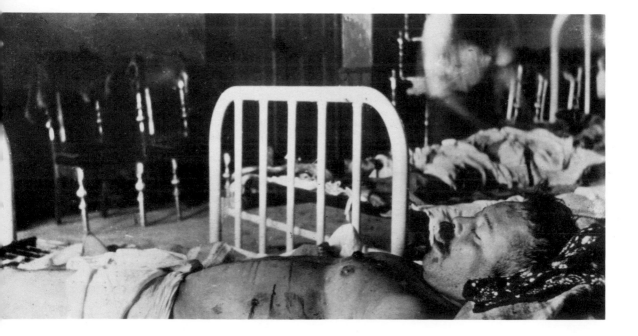

como campesino. La incapacidad del poderoso ejército estadounidense a capturarlo lo convirtieron en un símbolo de la habilidad del campesino mexicano de sobrevivir frente a condiciones sumamente desfavorables.

Una cosa está clara. Villa no se unió a la revolución para enriquecerse. En lugar de acumular el botín que conseguía como oficial rebelde, lo usaba para pagar a sus hombres y adquirir material militar. Económicamente, pudo haber ganado mucho más si hubiera continuado su existencia de bandido.

Probablemente, Villa se hizo revolucionario a causa de sus experiencias de joven. Sin duda, vengar los malos tratos a que fue sometido y el deseo de proteger a otros mexicanos pobres de esa misma suerte fueron factores importantes. A su manera, se mantuvo fiel a lo largo de su vida a Francisco Madero y a su dedicación al programa revolucionario de reforma.

Poco antes de su muerte, Villa le explicó con orgullo a un periodista que le visitaba que había establecido la pequeña escuela en su hacienda porque se daba cuenta de que las armas y la violencia nunca podrían lograr la reforma social. "Combatí durante diez años para que los pobres pudieran vivir como seres humanos ... Pero no valió gran cosa ... No se puede hacer nada hasta que se eduque al pueblo."

Pocas figuras en la historia moderna de México han atraído más a las masas que Pancho Villa. Fue la ironía de su vida que le traicionara un vendedor de la calle, alguien que pertenecía a la clase de la que procedía y cuya causa siempre había defendido con fervor.

CRONOLOGÍA

1878   Nace Doroteo Arango en Río Grande, México, el 5 de junio

1894   Asume el nombre Francisco "Pancho" Villa y se une a un grupo de proscritos; pasa la mayor parte de los próximos 16 años como bandido

1909   Se casa con María Luz Corral

1910   Los mexicanos se levantan contra el régimen de Porfirio Díaz; Villa se une al ejército revolucionario con el rango de capitán

1911   Las tropas de Villa toman Ciudad Juárez; la primera fase de la Revolución Mexicana acaba con el derrocamiento de Díaz; Francisco I. Madero es elegido presidente de México

1912   Villa defiende al gobierno de Madero de un intento de golpe; se le impone la condena de muerte por desobedencia; la pena se rebaja a dos años de cárcel; Villa se escapa y huye a El Paso, Tejas

1913   Madero es asesinado; Victoriano Huerta asume la presidencia; Villa jura vengar a Madero y se une a la alianza en contra de Huerta; toma Juárez y Chihuahua, convirtiéndose así en el amo del norte de México y una figura de fama internacional

1914   Las fuerzas de los Estados Unidos ocupan el puerto mexicano de Veracruz, presionando al régimen de Huerta; el ejército de Villa toma Zacatecas; Huerta dimite; Venustiano Carranza es presidente interino; Villa rompe con Carranza y forma una alianza con el líder campesino Emiliano Zapata; Villa y Zapata capturan la ciudad de México

1915   Villa se retira de la ciudad de México para batallar contra fuerzas pro-carrancistas en el norte; sufre derrotas a manos del General Obregón en Celaya y Aguascalientes; los Estados Unidos reconoce el régimen de Carranza como el gobierno legítimo de México y corta la ayuda a Villa; Villa sufre otra derrota en Agua Prieta

1916   Los villistas asaltan Columbus, Nuevo México; saquean el pueblo y matan a ciudadanos norteamericanos

1916-17   3,000 tropas estadounidenses persiguen sin éxito a Villa por las montañas del norte de México

1918   Villa reorganiza su ejército y resume sus ataques a los carrancistas

1919   El asalto de Villa a Juárez termina desastrosamente; su ejército es destrozado por tropas de los Estados Unidos que intervienen

1920   Cae el régimen de Carranza; Obregón es elegido presidente de México; Villa acepta una pensión y una hacienda de Obregón y se convierte en ranchero

1923   Es asesinado en Parral, México, el 20 de julio

Lectura adicional

Alonso Cortes, Rodrigo. *Francisco Villa, el quinto jinete del Apocalipis.* Tlacoqumécatl, México 12, D. F.: Editorial Diana, 1972.

Cervantes, Federico. *Francisco Villa y la revolución.* México 1, D. F.: Ediciones Alonso, 1960.

Herrera, Celia. *Francisco Villa ante la historia.* 2a ed. México, D. F.: s.n., 1964.

Krauze, Enrique. *Entre el ángel y el fierro: Francisco Villa.* México, D. F.: Fondo de Culture Económica, 1987.

Terrazas, Silvestre. *El verdadero Pancho Villa.* México, D. F.: Edicinones Era, 1985.

Vilanova Fuentes, Antonio. *Muerte de Villa.* México, D. F.: Editores Mexicanos Unidos, 1966.

ÍNDICE

STEVEN O'BRIEN enseñó temas sociales en las escuelas secundarias de Massachusetts durante casi 20 años. Recibió el título de M.A. de la Universidad de Connecticut, donde se especializó en historia; y un certificado de estudios avanzados además del título de Ph.D. de la Universidad de Harvard. Ha escrito para el *New York Times Magazine* y otras publicaciones, y es el autor de *Antonio López de Santa Anna* de la serie HISPANOS NOTABLES de Chelsea House. En la actualidad es el director de la Escuela de la Comunidad Americana en Atenas, Grecia.

RODOLFO CARDONA es Profesor de Español y Literatura Comparada de la Universidad de Boston. Investigador de renombre, ha escrito muchas obras de crítica, incluyendo *Ramón, a Study of Gómez de la Serna and His Works* (Ramón, un estudio de Gómez de la Serna y su obra) y *Visión del esperpento: Teoría y práctica del esperpento en Valle-Inclán*. Nació en San José, Costa Rica, hizo su licenciatura y maestría en la Universidad del Estado de Louisiana y recibió un Doctorado en Filosofía y Letras en la Universidad de Washington. Ha enseñado en la Universidad de Case Western Reserve, la Universidad de Pittsburgh, la Universidad de Texas en Austin, la Universidad de New Mexico y la Universidad de Harvard.

JAMES COCKCROFT es actualmente Profesor Visitante de Estudios Latinoamericanos y del Caribe de la Universidad de Nueva York en Albany. Tres veces ganador de la beca Fullbright, recibió su doctorado de la Universidad de Stanford y ha enseñado en la Universidad de Massachusetts, la Universidad de Vermont, y la Universidad de Connecticut. Es autor o co-autor de numerosos libros sobre asuntos latinoamericanos, incluyendo *Neighbor in Turmoil: Latin America* (Vecinos en confusión: La América Latina), *The Hispanic Experience in the United States: Contemporary Issues and Perspectives* (La experiencia hispana en los Estados Unidos: Problemas y perspectivas del momento), y *Outlaws in the Promised Land: Mexican Immigrant Workers and America's Future* (Foragidos en la tierra prometida: Obreros inmigrantes mexicanos y el futuro de América).

40	91.22
Zr	
Zirconium	

THE GENE FORRESTER JAIL IS THE UGLIEST BUILDING IN TOWN. ITS concrete facade is covered in black soot as though a fire once engulfed the Gene, but there was no fire because fires do not break out here. We do not even have matches. In my first month in heaven, I often tried lighting a leaf on fire using a magnifying glass and a sunray, but the experiments proved fruitless. Only a thin wisp of smoke ever emerged.

The windows at the Gene are barred, so it is lucky that buildings do not catch on fire. Another unusual thing about this four-story building is its shape: a perfect cube. Most buildings I have seen are rectangular. Also, the Gene has no exterior architectural features. No awnings or cornices, for example.

I wonder who the inmates are. They must be townies who have committed offenses like serious acts of vandalism, disturbances of the peace, and violence causing injury. Such offenses are rare here, though. Perhaps Zig subdues certain townies in order to make the most wicked of dead American thirteen-year-olds a bit kinder and to avoid bloody clashes in Town.

I get off my bicycle and tie a red ribbon around the handlebars. The day is sunny and the sky the azure color that you, Father, call wild blue yonder. It is the kind of day when you, Mother, would remind me to wear a sun hat.

As I have mentioned, our skin never burns in heaven. Yet I do feel sunburned after my two-hour bicycle ride. Maybe I am suffering from heatstroke and should look for a water fountain. I stumble up the steps of the building into the Gene's lobby, where a long wooden desk is manned by identical twin boys whose name stickers read, TIM LU and TOM LU. They are both wearing T-shirts with a yin-yang decal. I surmise they died in an accident like a house fire or a car crash. Their passing at the same time is lucky in an odd way; after all, losing a twin must be like losing a part of yourself.

The Lu twins are reading twin copies of *The Swiss Family Robinson*. "Greetings. My name is Oliver Dalrymple. I am here to visit an inmate," I tell them. "A boy named Johnny Henzel."

"Did he say Johnny Henzel?" Tim says to Tom.

"Yes, oh my, he did," Tom says. "He *did* say Johnny Henzel." I nod.

"The boy who came in last night," Tim says to Tom as they both put down their books.

"The Grade F."

"We *never* have Grade F's. When was the last one, Tom?"

"Before our time, I'm sure. Decades ago."

"What does 'Grade F' mean?" I ask.

"Oliver Dalrymple doesn't know what 'Grade F' means."

"Of course he doesn't. He's an outsider. 'Grade F' is an insider term. It means Johnny Henzel did something really, really bad."

"Heinous, you might say."

"Yes, heinous or even egregious."

The twins do not look at me while they talk. They look at and speak to each other.

"I wonder what he could have done," Tom says.

"Maybe he kidnapped somebody," Tim replies. "We haven't had a kidnapper in ages, have we, Tom?"

"No, I can't recall the last one."

"But kidnappers are usually classified as Grade D."

"Maybe it was a series of kidnappings."

"Oh my, a serial kidnapper," Tim says. "How despicable."

I cut in: "Johnny Henzel is not a serial kidnapper. He hit a boy over the head with a flashlight."

"A flashlight?" Tim says to Tom. "That isn't Grade F. That is Grade B, or at most C, depending on the injuries."

"Also, it is alleged he shot somebody to death back in America."

"Murder!!!!" Tom shouts.

"Keep it down, Tom! You're not being very professional."

"Murder is definitely Grade F."

"Could I see Johnny Henzel?" I say.

"Oliver Dalrymple wants to visit a Grade F!"

"Even Grade D's can't have visitors. Even Grade D's are in solitary confinement on the fourth floor. So imagine Grade F's!"

"But I am the boy who Johnny allegedly shot."

"Oliver Dalrymple's the victim! Oh my! Oh goodness! A shooting victim!"

"Well, this is highly unusual, don't you think, Tim?"

" 'Unprecedented' is the word that leaps to mind."

Tim and Tom Lu converse back and forth like this before deciding that one of them will check with authorities to see if Johnny can receive a visit from the boy he shot.

"*Allegedly* shot," I say as Tim pushes back his chair and heads off.

While Tim is gone, I sit on a bench in a far corner and stare at the colored floor tiles, which form a kind of circular mandala like those that Buddhist monks create out of sand. Mandalas are supposed to favor peace, but my state of mind is hardly peaceful.

People who believe in a god often think, during trying periods in their lives, that their god is testing them. Is Zig conducting some kind of experiment here in Town despite his usual hands-off policy?

Rover has disappeared. I hope the roach was not trampled to death in the melee last night.

I rush back outside and hop on my bike. The trip ahead will be a long jaunt requiring me to wind through a labyrinth of streets and to cross four zones (Five, One, Two, Nine). I tell myself to focus on the road. I must not become careless and smash into a streetlamp or another cyclist. I do not want to end up in an infirmary with a concussion, which, according to my notes, takes from four to six days to heal.

Still, my mind does wander. I keep picturing the hallway of Helen Keller in the first seconds after the gun went off and everybody in the hall—except the boy who pulled the trigger and the boy who was struck by the bullet—turned toward the bang. What did my classmates and teachers see?

My mind's eye imagines everyone and everything frozen in the moment. Henry Axworthy bends over the drinking fountain, an arc of water suspended before him. Jermaine Tucker drops his math book, but it does not hit the floor. Patsy Hyde's lips peel back in a scream, exposing the braces she usually keeps hidden. Cynthia Orwell dribbles a basketball that hovers a foot from her hand. The art teacher, Mr. Huston, holds a still-life drawing he is set to tape to the wall outside his classroom. Helen Keller, as always, sits posed with a mortarboard on her head in her portrait hung across from locker No. 106.

Their eyes are all turned in the same direction.

There seems to be a blind spot in my imagination, because though I see everything else perfectly, even my crumpled body at the foot of my locker, there is one thing my mind's eye cannot make out in the hallway: the face of the boy holding the gun.

After ten minutes, Tim Lu is still not back. Meanwhile, the front doors to the Gene open, and in come Reginald Washington and Sandy Goldberg. They walk with purpose, their running shoes squeaking across the mandala. Reginald takes out his official do-good council president badge. They speak to Tom Lu, who says, "Boy, is our Grade F a popular boy today. There's a lineup to see him." Tom nods toward the bench where I sit. I stand as Reginald and Sandy turn toward me.

Reginald narrows his eyes. He looks peeved. "Heaven help us," he says, loudly enough for me to hear. He crosses the floor to speak to me.

"Hello, Oliver," he says, a forced smile on his face. "What a surprise to see you here."

"I want to see Johnny," I say.

His smile disappears. "Did Thelma send you? What was that girl thinking?"

"I want to be the one giving Johnny the news."

Reginald slowly shakes his head. "No can do, brother. No can do."

"Why not? I am his friend. One of his few friends here."

Reginald pats my shoulder. "You've had a shock," he says. "You need to rest in peace. In fact, I've asked Thelma to book you into the Deborah."

"The asylum?!" I picture Willa Blake's sickening plunge from the roof. "That is the last place I need to be!"

Reginald tells me I can wait in the lobby till he and Sandy finish their business upstairs with Johnny and the authorities. "Afterward, I'd like to talk to you about acting as a witness in a trial," he says.

He returns to speak with the Lu twins. I feel exhausted. I press the palms of my hands into my eyes, just as I used to do in America when my eyes were red from reading mathematics books for hours on end. When I remove them, Sandy stands before me.

"Hello again, Oliver. You sure made good time. Reginald and me stopped along the way for blueberry pancakes. There was no butter, though. I totally miss butter, and I wish Zig would send us some, but at least we got syrup, right? Imagine if Zig decided, 'No sweets for my children.'" She does Zig's voice low and gruff. "'Their teeth will rot out of their head!' That would be a tragedy and a half, don't you think? Having no sweets, I mean. Not rotten teeth. Are you a butter person?"

I have the unkind thought that her brain is the size of the peanut that did her in. "May I ask you a question?" I say.

"Sure, ask away. I'm an open book."

"Did Johnny Henzel target me back at Helen Keller Junior High? When he shot his gun, did he plan to hit *me*?"

I cannot stop myself from asking, even though my question implies that I believe Johnny is guilty.

Sandy shrugs. "I hardly remember a thing, just that the other kid was in a psycho ward. I remember that 'cause I almost got sent to a psycho ward once. My mom thought I was anorexic—can you believe it?—but the reason I didn't eat much was 'cause I was just always afraid of swallowing an allergen. I was allergic to loads of things—nuts, strawberries, buckwheat, tomatoes. But nuts were totally the worst. I couldn't even—"

"You hardly remember a thing?!" I say, my voice rising and going squeaky. "One must be absolutely certain with accusations such as yours, Ms. Goldberg!"

She shrugs again, and I finally understand the phrase "shooting the messenger" because I want to slap her silly face.

Reginald comes back. "We have to go now, Sandy," he says.

"Tell Johnny I'm here," I plead with them. "Give him a message from me. Tell him . . ."

What to tell him? *Do not lose hope. Do not lose your mind.*

"Tell him, 'If you're ever in a jam, here I am.'"

It is a line from the song "Friendship."

Tim Lu has returned and says loudly to his brother, "Until further notice, Mr. Dalrymple is denied the right to visit the Grade F."

Because of his council president badge, however, Reginald is not denied visiting rights. Tom Lu escorts him and Sandy to the staircase leading to the upper floors.

When they are gone, I tell myself I must be as hardy as Joe and Frank: I must concoct a plan to rescue Johnny from this place. I sit back down. I am so dog-tired that my body, seemingly without my brain's consent, lies across the bench. Thelma had given me a hooded sweatshirt to wear over my T-shirt, and I take it off to use as a pillow under my head. Tim and Tom throw me scolding looks from behind their novels, but I do not, as Johnny would say, give a flying f*ck (an expression whose etymology I cannot even guess).

Nobody else comes in or goes out. The jail seems to be the most undcrused building in heaven. It is so quiet that I wonder if I might hear Johnny's reaction when he learns of the charges against him.

It is unfathomable to me that Johnny Henzel was Gunboy on the fourth day of eighth grade at Helen Keller Junior High. It simply cannot be. But even if it were true, I tell myself, it should not matter. What should matter is whether Johnny is Gunboy now, here in our heaven reserved for American thirteen-year-olds.

The front door of the jail opens. In walks Esther, wearing a pink beret. I sit up. She spots me right away and waves. I am heartened to see her. I wave back.

41 — **92.91** — **Nb** — Niobium

42 — **95.95** — **Mo** — Molybdenum

43 — **[97.91]** — **Tc** — Technetium

44   101.07

Ru

Ruthenium

IT IS NEW YEAR'S EVE DAY, THE LAST DAY OF THE SEVENTIES. IT has been three weeks since I last saw Johnny. When I pass by the Gene's backyard, I gaze up at the windows on the fourth floor, but they are tiny—barely larger than the cover of a comic book. I cannot see whether anyone is looking out. I am not even sure which room Johnny is held in.

It can be upsetting to come here because a posse of demonstrators often gathers in the yard. I do not know why the jailers allow this. Maybe they see the demonstrations as a form of just punishment. The demonstrators, mostly gommers, from what I gather, carry placards scrawled with hurtful messages, such as JOHNNY HENZEL YOUR AN ERROR.

The worst placard I have seen, however, was wielded by Benny Baggarly, the gommer who turned Johnny and me in to the do-good authorities. His placard contained two words in big letters: REDEATH PENALTY!

Since today is a holiday, the demonstrators are not here when Esther and I show up at the Gene. I bring along a placard made from a broom handle and a piece of poster board. Esther suggested I communicate with Johnny this way. I did not know what to say. On my placard, I finally wrote, IN THE PURSUIT OF TRUTH WE ARE PERMITTED TO REMAIN CHILDREN ALL OUR LIVES. It is a quote from Albert Einstein. I hope it is not too obscure. I simply mean to say I will keep an open mind and get to the bottom of the mystery surrounding us.

Esther has come with me, but she has gone into the lobby

to speak to Tim and Tom Lu. They give her whispered updates on the boy they still refer to only as "the Grade F." They refuse to give updates to me. They are wary of me. They call me the victim. "Oh, the victim's back again," Tim might say. And Tom might reply, "When will that boy learn he isn't welcome here?"

As I wait for Esther, I stand in the yard behind the jail, my placard raised. The windows on the lower floors are normal-size. In one window, I notice a jailbird with an orange baseball cap. He waves to me, and I wave my sign back.

Holy mackerel clouds are rolling across the sky this afternoon. They are Johnny's favorite, so perhaps he is peeking out his tiny window right now.

I am so absorbed in the thought that I do not at first notice that Esther has returned. She is furrowing her brow.

"What?" I say.

She bites her top lip and shakes her head grimly. Then she says, "That stupid b*stard hasn't touched his food in a week now."

"Johnny is not eating?"

"He's on a hunger strike."

I glance back at the Gene.

"He'll start eating again on one condition," she says. "If he's allowed a visit from you."

TOWNIES CAN STOP EATING ALL THEY WANT, BUT THEY WILL never grow thinner. Thelma went on a drastic diet early in her stay in Town, but she says she simply grew so weak she started hallucinating (toucans flocking in the trees and dolphins swimming through the clouds). Whether we can die from abstaining from food nobody seems to know, because nobody—not even a sadcon at the Deborah—has stopped eating long enough.

The hypnotist Charles "Czar" Lindblom is no longer in a coma, and once he started coming around, he was fed the types of food a baby eats: mashed potatoes, applesauce, gruel. He is now strong enough to serve as a witness at Johnny's trial, which gets under way in a week's time.

It feels lonely having my room to myself. I am glad Johnny left many of his drawings behind to adorn the walls. He did a series called *Wish Come True*. For example, there is one drawing of Thelma dressed in pearls and a sparkly gown like the dress a jazz singer might wear onstage.

He asked me to choose a subject for my own portrait. I told him to give me time to decide on a suitable wish. Were he here now, I would ask him to draw the two of us lying in the snow in Hoffman Estates and gazing at the wispy moon. In that moment, we were truly resting in peace.

Around seven o'clock, Thelma and Esther knock on my door because we are supposed to go to a play together. Plenty of plays, concerts, magic shows, choreographies, and acrobatics will be staged tonight. You see, on New Year's Eve, townies present the most beautiful art they created in the past year. All across Town, painters exhibit their finest paintings, and sculptors their best sculptures. Guitarists play the compositions that make them proudest. Harpists strum their most angelic pieces. Singers sing their most heartrending songs. Poets stand on soapboxes and recite their most elegant poems, and storywriters read aloud their most inspired work. Townies claim they do all these things to thank Zig, but I believe they are also trying to prove they are bearing up well despite the box (i.e., the terrarium) that their god has confined them to.

Just after we leave the Frank and Joe, Esther turns to Thelma and me in the street. She is wearing a fake mink stole, what she calls her "fun fur." "Let's make a pact," she says. "That tonight we won't talk about it."

Thelma nods in agreement. "We need a break, at least for a few hours."

"Okay," I say, even though I feel like a traitor.

The play we will see is called *The Effect of Gamma Rays on Man-in-the-Moon Marigolds*. Thelma says it is about a girl awe-struck by science and mistreated by her crazy mother. It is right up our alley because I am fond of science and Esther had an overbearing mother (who nicknamed her daughter Li'l, a name Esther loathed).

We head down the street, which is teeming with bicycles and pedestrians. Everybody seems to be out this evening. Townies sing aloud and do dance steps on the sidewalk. A boy does a triple cartwheel across the lawn of his dorm and then a somersault in the air. Do-gooders climb trees in a park to hang balloons and streamers from the branches.

Exhibition tables are set up along the sidewalks. At one table sits a boy who creates origami creatures (tiger, grasshopper, giraffe, pterodactyl) and silver necklaces like those that children in America make out of gum wrappers (Town has no gum, so he uses aluminum foil). Beside him is a girl who makes shoebox dioramas of scenes from novels (for example, a jungle scene from *Tarzan of the Apes*). Beside her is a boy who makes papier-mâché masks, one of which has a schnozzola like Uncle Seymour's.

A girl with hair that looks cut with a Weedwacker comes up to me in the street. "You're Boo, right?" she says. "The murdered kid?" People recognize me lately, though there are no newspapers or television reports here to display my photograph.

"Just want to say," she says with a shy smile, "that I'm rooting for you." She places a hand on my shoulder, but Esther brushes it off for me.

"Rooting for me," I say. "What do you mean?"

"Well, the kid who shot you, I think he really should get—"

Thelma cuts in: "We're late for a play."

The girl goes on: "His just deserts."

I do not know how to reply, so I concentrate on etymology. "The expression 'just deserts' doesn't mean the cake or cookie we eat after a meal," I tell the girl. "It means what a person justly deserves."

The girl blinks at me. "Yeah, I know. And your killer deserves to be hung." She does a pantomime of tightening a noose around her own neck.

Thelma pats her heart.

"The correct past participle is 'hanged,'" I say.

"We're not talking about it tonight!" Esther yells at the girl, her arms gesturing wildly. "So shut your big fat ignorant mouth!"

The girl backs away as though Esther is a snarling dog.

This brief encounter seems to ruin any pretense of a festive mood. On the rest of our walk to the theater, the three of us speak little. Luckily, however, the play turns out to be excellent. In it, a girl named Tillie Hunsdorfer exposes marigolds to radioactivity. Some of the flowers wither and die, while others mutate into odd but splendid creatures.

Thelma has warned us she often cries at the theater, and she does in fact weep during the final scene where Tillie's mother murders Tillie's pet rabbit. Esther hands Thelma tissues from her purse, which is decorated with felt sunflowers.

I, of course, do not weep. I am not used to attending plays. In America, as you know, Mother and Father, I did not go to the theater. I did not watch situation comedies or police dramas on television. I did not read novels. I did not do any of the things requiring a leap into a fictional world. I did not understand the need for fiction when real-life events—the true dramas occurring at the cellular level in our bodies and at the astrophysical level in our universe—were so fantastic and fascinating.

Only in the real world of heaven have I discovered a use for make-believe. One benefit of fiction: it puts your mind off your reality when your reality is off-putting. I wish I had made this discovery back in America. Maybe *Lord of the Flies* would have helped me survive junior high.

When the play is over and we are discussing the merits of its fictional world in the lobby of the school, we are brought back to reality by a poster thumbtacked to a cork bulletin board. The title of the poster reads, THE SON OF THE SON OF SAM.

It is about Johnny. His crimes. His upcoming trial. The local gommer group is urging townies to demonstrate outside the Gene throughout the trial. I read aloud: "'A bloodthirsty killer is in our midst and may strike again if we do not—'"

Esther rips down the poster and crumples it before I can read to the end. "Damn gommers," she says, narrowing her eyes at Thelma. Thelma has in fact been kicked out of the local gommer group because she wavers on the need to punish crimes committed before a townie passed into heaven. The word around Town is that if Johnny is found guilty, the gommers are pushing for a public stoning.

"I wish we could get away from heaven," Thelma says. "I wish we could go on a haunting to my grandma's house in Louisiana. We could pick peaches and make a pie. We could save a slice for Johnny to end his hunger strike."

Esther rolls her eyes at the idea. "Oh, for f*ck sake," she says, adopting Johnny's expression.

Thelma looks dejected, and I probably look sad and confused.

"You two deadbeats need to cheer the hell up," Esther says. "It's New Year's Eve!"

"I'm scared what'll happen," Thelma whispers. "Gommers gunning for a stoning. Johnny not eating."

"Our pact!" Esther cries, hands on hips.

We go sit under a weeping willow in a park. Around us, revelers play flutes, harmonicas, and Jew's harps. People sing show tunes, disco songs, and jazz standards. I ask the girls about their plans for the New Year.

Thelma will put together a musical on the life of Miss Otis from the Cole Porter song. She will write, direct, and star. Because Miss Otis was crazy, Thelma will call the musical *Out to Lunch*.

Esther will design clothes for other fashionable townies using the sewing machine in her room. Her tastes run to high fashion, so she will make items like pleated skirts and ruffled blouses. She will knit sweater vests out of acrylic yarn. She also has "a hippie, groovy side" and will draw dozens of peace symbols with a Magic Marker on a canvas belt and bouquets of daisies on a vinyl purse.

I tell the girls I plan to write a guide to grammar and punctuation titled *Who Is Whom?* I may also take some literature classes. Students learn about the history of the American South by reading *Huckleberry Finn* and *Tom Sawyer*. They learn about the Roaring Twenties by reading *The Great Gatsby* and *The Sun Also Rises*. They learn about justice by reading *To Kill a Mockingbird*. They learn some French by reading *Tintin*.

I will also start work part-time at Curios right after the holiday. Peter Peter wants me to help him with a new exhibition spotlighting curious townies, late thirteen-year-olds who made a name for themselves in odd ways in their afterlife.

For example, the late Frederick Koenig was a big-calved boy who, for nine years in a row, won the Tour de Paradis, a bicycle race along the streets bordering the four Great Walls.

The late Diego Alvarez, a baker's son, became Town's most celebrated chef. He whipped up mouthwatering recipes that most townies had never tasted before, like stuffed charred peppers, maple butternut soup, and portobello mushroom risotto. He left behind a cookbook titled *Diego's Diner*.

The late Lesley Gapper was a postmistress who came up with the zip codes assigned to the different blocks in the thirteen zones. Each code is a three-letter pronounceable word, like HAM, ROW, TIP, and GUT. As a result, people living on the different blocks sometimes call themselves hammers, rowers, tippers, and gutters.

On the subject of neologisms, the late Monica Schneider created a glossary of heavenisms, words coined here or used differently here than in America. She typed dozens and dozens of copies of her glossary to distribute. The words include "townie," "gommer," "do-gooder," "sadcon," "old boy," and another I have learned recently, "countdowner."

A countdowner is somebody who stands on a rooftop on New Year's Eve and counts down minutes and seconds while

townies gather around to shout "Thank Zig!" simultaneously
when the clock strikes midnight.

In fact, I will be the countdowner at the Frank and Joe
tonight, so the girls and I walk back to my dorm. We head
to the roof, where a dozen townies are wandering about with
flashlights or penlights in their hands. Gym mats are spread
everywhere so we can lie and gaze at Zig's sky as we await the
spiritual moment when we will all thank our god and the lucky
stars he gave us.

Over the next half hour, more and more townies appear on
the roof of the Frank and Joe—not only residents but also guests
from other dorms. All around me people choose a gym mat and
lie down. Esther and Thelma do likewise on either side of me.
As tonight's countdowner, I am the only person allowed to stay
standing. I am also the only person permitted to speak before
the time comes to give thanks. I stand between Esther and
Thelma, a hand grasping a bullhorn and my eyes on my glow-
in-the-dark ghost. When Casper's little hand points north and
his big hand hits ten, I shout into the bullhorn: *"Ten minutes!"*
An echo sweeps over us because countdowners all across Town
are yelling the same thing, our wristwatches synchronized.

I stare skyward and picture you, Mother, with your smile
that exposes your gums, and you, Father, with your eyelids that
droop when you are tired.

I get lost in my thoughts and miss my Casper cue. *"Five
minutes!"* comes the call from surrounding buildings. Shoot! I
make my announcement, but a few seconds late.

I look up at my three-legged horse hovering in the stars.
While I stare at my constellation, the stars forming its tail start
to move. I blink several times, but they keep moving back and
forth as though the horse is wagging its tail like a dog. Goose
bumps rise on my arms. Is this a spiritual moment?

"Zig?" I whisper in the night.

I glance down at Esther and Thelma. By now all flashlights are off, so I cannot make out their expressions. Do they see the wagging stars? Does anyone else? Nobody around me seems startled or alarmed. Everyone gazes heavenward. There is barely a sound, other than an occasional cough or sneeze and the skin of people's limbs unsticking now and then from the vinyl mats.

I check Casper just in time. *"One minute!"* I shout together with countdowners atop all the surrounding dorms.

I glance back at the horse, but its tail has come to a rest, fixed again in the heavens. My eyes must be playing tricks on me tonight.

Throughout Town, hundreds and hundreds of reborn thirteen-year-olds prepare to thank Zig for their life after death. In fact, we townies form a kind of Milky Way, each of us a star in a galaxy of Zig's making. Esther Haglund, Thelma Rudd, Peter Peterman, Reginald Washington, Tim and Tom Lu, Charles Lindblom, Sandy Goldberg, and of course Johnny Henzel.

The final countdown begins. Into my bullhorn, I shout: *"Ten Mississippi! Nine Mississippi! Eight Mississippi! Seven Mississippi! Six Mississippi! Five Mississippi! Four Mississippi! Three Mississippi! Two Mississippi! One Mississippi!"*

Off go all the streetlamps as a roar rises into the night skies. A flare erupting from the mouth of every boy and every girl across the land. A cry that is meant to be gratitude but that sounds strangely like anger.

"THANK ZIG!"

TWO DAYS AFTER NEW YEAR'S, I AM IN MY NEW OFFICE ON THE
third floor of the Guy Montag Library when there comes a
knock at my door. I expect it is the curator, Peter Peter.

Peter Peter has gone through puberty, can grow some facial
hair, and speaks with a deep voice; he may look like the kind
of strapping boy who used to taunt me back at Helen Keller,
but he is in fact kind and patient. Sometimes I lunch with the
old boy and quiz him about the forty-six years he has spent in
heaven. Peter Peter is a true anthropologist, an expert on the
evolution of Town and the objects sent here. He calls me son.
He is older than you, Father.

On New Year's Day, he invited Thelma to a harpsichord concert in the Northeast Corner (where the North and East Walls
meet). Thelma now says they are going steady, even though
Esther says one date does not sound steady to her.

I put down the object I am studying—a silver cigarette
lighter with a rattlesnake engraved on its side—and go open
my office door. It is not Peter Peter after all. To my surprise, it
is Tim and Tom Lu. Over their T-shirts, they wear contrasting
neckties: Tim's is blue with red polka dots, and Tom's is red with
blue polka dots.

"Tom, you have a message to deliver to the victim, don't
you?"

"I certainly do, Tim. A private, sealed letter from Lydia Finkle, the jail warden."

"I wonder what the letter says," Tim replies.

"I asked Ms. Finkle myself, but she pretended not to hear me," Tom says.

"Maybe the victim will open his letter and read it aloud so we'll know what Ms. Finkle wants with him."

As usual, they do not look directly at me while they speak. Tim hands a manila envelope to Tom, who hands it back to Tim. They pass the envelope back and forth till finally I reach over and pluck it away.

"I wonder if it hurts to get shot in the back."

"If your friend is the shooter, I imagine it hurts very much."

"The word 'agonizing' might apply."

"I'd go so far as to say 'excruciating.'"

I walk over to my desk and use my fake-tortoiseshell letter opener on the envelope. I pull out the letter, unfold it, and read it aloud to satisfy the twins.

Dear Oliver Dalrymple,

In my capacity as warden of the Gene Forrester Jail, I am writing to request your presence at our facility this Wednesday at ten in the morning.

I have been informed you wish to visit one of our prisoners, John Henzel, who would not be permitted a visitor under normal circumstances, given the seriousness of the accusations weighing against him. However, as I am sure you are well aware, the circumstances in this particular case are far from normal.

Mr. Henzel has foolishly embarked upon a hunger strike as his trial draws near. He has informed us that he will resume eating if allowed a visit from you. After much reflection, the board here at the jail, together with the do-good council from your own zone, has agreed to consent to Mr. Henzel's request. Please note, however, that your visit will be supervised by your council president, Mr. Reginald Washington, and limited to ten minutes.

I feel we must all work together to ensure Mr. Henzel remains fit and lucid enough to attend his trial. Can I count on your presence then this coming Wednesday? Please send me an immediate reply through my couriers.

> Yours sincerely,
> Lydia Finkle
> Warden, Gene Forrester Jail

I go to the typewriter on my desk and remove the description of butane (C_4H_{10}) that I was writing. I crank in a blank sheet of paper and reply to Lydia Finkle.

Dear Lydia Finkle,

Thank you for your invitation to visit Johnny Henzel. You can certainly count on my presence on Wednesday.

Before meeting you in person, however, I wish to inform you of certain facts, not about the accusations weighing against Johnny (I am sure you are familiar with those), but rather regarding my own reaction to the possibility he ended my life back in America.

The friends I have made here in heaven (and even strangers who have heard my story) all wish to know how I feel now about Johnny.

Ms. Finkle, I can assure you I do not feel vengeful or spiteful. People ask if I can forgive Johnny, but "forgive" and "forgiveness" are not words I would use in this case because I have never felt anger toward him.

What I feel is mercy. I feel merciful toward him because

if he did commit the crime in question, he did so during a psychotic rage that bears no relation to the boy who now sits in your jail cell.

Most gommers expect me to share their desire for an eye for an eye and a tooth for a tooth. They believe if I do not feel vengeful for my own death, I should at least feel vengeful for theirs (many of their murders were indeed horrific). In other words, they want to borrow my eye and my tooth so they can then feel free to pluck out Johnny's. I do not deem such a response fair to anyone.

Death changes a child. We townies are not necessarily the same children we left behind in our previous lives. I myself am slightly less intelligent and slightly more social than the boy I left crumpled on the floor of a school hallway in Hoffman Estates, Illinois. Owing to this change in character, I can feel for another human being, something I admit I had trouble doing back in America.

I can feel friendship and I can feel mercy.

Ms. Finkle, you also must be different today from the person you once were. Maybe in America you were a vain and haughty girl devoted to collecting cashmere sweaters and Girl Scouts badges. (This is just a guess on my part based on girls I knew in Illinois.)

In any event, I expect you are wiser than the thirteen-year-old girl you left behind. I imagine that, to serve as warden, you must have great wisdom. Can I count on your wisdom to treat Johnny Henzel with mercy?

> Kind regards,
> Oliver "Boo" Dalrymple

By the time I finish typing, Tim and Tom Lu are sitting on the floor of my office and playing Go Fish with a deck of cards adorned with images of bare-breasted ladies (a curious object that came in from Two yesterday). I hand over my typed letter and tell them to read it if they wish. They do so, shoulder to shoulder, their lips moving silently in tandem.

When they finish, Tim says to Tom, "Would you show mercy to me if I murdered you?"

Tom replies, "Are you crazy? Not on your life!"

PRISONERS MUST DRESS IN ORANGE T-SHIRTS, ORANGE GYM shorts, and orange sneakers so they are easier to recognize should they escape. Townies tend not to dress in all-orange clothing to avoid looking like a prisoner, but Esther brought me a similar orange getup to wear in solidarity during my visit to the Gene. When Tim Lu sees my outfit, he says, "Oh, how adorable, the victim identifies with the Grade F." Tom Lu unlocks the door leading inside the jail and takes me down a series of hallways. I carry a peach pie, which Thelma made for Johnny to entice him to start eating again.

The building's interior looks as though an earthquake of at least six on the Richter scale has struck. Usually buildings can repair themselves, but the Gene certainly seems less efficient in this regard. Doorways are so crooked that doors are beveled to close properly, deep cracks run across walls, patches of plaster are missing from ceilings, floorboards are loose and squeaky, and nail heads jut out of them to trip us up. "Watch your step," Tom says, pointing out a nail head or two. He leads me past the offices of the prison guards, who wear their purple armbands. At the end of another hall is a door marked WARDEN.

Tom knocks and calls out, "Ms. Finkle, Mr. Merciful is here." He leads me into the office but does not leave till the warden shoos him away. Lydia Finkle is a doe-faced, straw-haired girl. She wears a sweatshirt inside out so the fluffy cashmere-like side is exposed. Pinned to her sweater is a badge illustrating a campfire. I do not know how to interpret these direct references to my letter. Is she being flippant or supportive? She sits in a swivel chair cranked to its highest height, and consequently her feet do not touch the floor. She is swinging them, and I wish she would stop.

Reginald Washington is also here. I tell myself not to stare at his splotchy skin, but it is difficult because I find his vitiligo beautiful. It reminds me of a jigsaw puzzle or an island nation such as Malaysia. The council president is wearing a striped necktie over an $E = mc^2$ T-shirt. He also has a lime-colored pick wedged into his Afro.

He is perched on one end of a threadbare couch and motions for me to sit too. I take a seat on the opposite end and hold the pie in my lap. The pie contains a nail file because Esther insisted Johnny could use a little levity. Esther and Thelma are waiting in the lobby and have suggested certain things to tell Johnny. He should stay hopeful, for instance, because we will do our utmost to free him. He should stick to the truth at his trial. The jury, we are sure, will realize he is no longer the boy he might have been in America.

Reginald says to me, "I want you to know I am personally opposed to this meeting. It sets a dangerous precedent."

The warden sighs and stops swinging her feet. "Oh, Reginald," she says. "Let's not go down that road again."

"It's a form of blackmail," he says, wagging a finger at her.

I turn to my council president. "How did you feel when you first came to Town?" I ask. "Did you come here different from the boy you used to be? Did Zig change you in any way? Did he make you more confident? More adjusted? I imagine a boy with your condition must have attracted his share of cruelty back in America."

Reginald exhales dramatically. "What is your point, Oliver?" he says. "That Zig adjusts all of us for the better? That he did the same for John Henzel? Well, that's your opinion, one that other people—like a certain Charles Lindblom—may not share."

The warden cuts in: "Reginald, we shouldn't say what other witnesses may or may not think."

Reginald gives her a pouty look.

"We should proceed with the visit," the warden says. "The Grade F is waiting."

So we rise, and the warden extends her hand to me. I shake it quickly. Her palm is dry, as though she rubs chalk dust over it. "I *was* a fan of cashmere," she says, looking me in the eye. "But that was another lifetime ago when I was a very different kind of girl."

Reginald guides me through the hallways of the ground floor to a staircase leading to the upper floors. When we reach the fourth floor, I get a sinking feeling because I notice that heavy furniture has been placed in front of certain doors. The doors are not barred like in a jail in America. They are the same kind of solid wooden doors found in any dorm in heaven.

As we walk down the hall, one prisoner shouts from his room, "Hey, you guys, I need clean sheets. I wet the bed again."

Three jailers in armbands slide a dresser away from Johnny's door. One jailer is Ringo, the British fellow who dragged me out of the gymnasium. He nods at me and says, "You watch yourself in there. That chap is unpredictable. He threw his breakfast tray at me this morning. I brought him another one."

Once the dresser is out of the way, Reginald taps on the door. "Hello there, John. It's President Washington. I'm here with your visitor."

Reginald unlocks the simple push-button doorknob, swings the door open, and strides inside.

Johnny Henzel is sitting on a mattress placed directly on the concrete floor near the far wall. I feel both glad and glum—glad because here he is, alive and kicking, and glum because he looks paler than I.

"I'll be your countdowner," Reginald says. "I'll wait here in the doorway and time your visit."

Johnny motions me over and pats the mattress. I kick off my running shoes and join him there. He is wearing the standard orange shorts and T-shirt, and orange-ringed socks. His eyes are dark and sunken, his lips dry and cracked. He runs a hand through his bristly hair.

"Hey, Boo," he says, his voice hoarser than on the night he arrived in Town. "What's new?"

"Hello, Johnny."

I set the peach pie on the floor beside a plastic tray containing a bowl of Raisin Bran, a glass of carrot juice, an apple, and a few figs on a paper plate. Maybe this will be the meal he will eat at the end of our visit. Beside the tray is a sketch pad, along with a wooden cigar box.

I wonder if I should hug Johnny. I am usually allergic to hugs, but ought I make an exception? Johnny gives me a guarded look, as though he is a little afraid of me, or shy.

The room is the same size as our dorm room at the Frank and Joe, but other than a small chair-desk, there is no furniture. A few orange T-shirts are stacked in a corner with balled-up socks piled atop them. The walls are crisscrossed with cracks. The tiny window is too high to look out of, and I suppose it does not slide open. Off the main room is a closet-size space containing a toilet and a pedestal sink.

"Listen, Boo," Johnny whispers, leaning close. He does not smell oniony, so the jailers must prod him into showering. "Take a peek inside my pencil case. There's something I want you to see, but I don't want the jailers to know about it. Understand?"

I glance at the cigar box. Various dog breeds are printed on it: poodles, Great Danes, boxers.

"Yeah, they let me draw in the slammer," he says a little louder so Reginald can hear. "I'd go nuts if I couldn't draw."

I pick up the box. I lift the lid.

Heavens! Inside, sitting on a raft of colored pencils, is *Blaberus craniifer*.

I shut the box. Johnny takes it from me.

My eyebrows raise. "How?" I say.

"He came out of my sink," Johnny whispers, nodding toward his bathroom. "He followed me here like a lost dog tracking down his master. The jailers don't know. They can't know or they'll take him away."

"Seven minutes!" Reginald calls out from his post in the doorway. He is like a zoologist observing the behavior of two monkeys placed in the same cage.

"Rover has helped me find a portal."

"A portal?" I whisper back.

"I'm getting out of here," he says in an urgent whisper. "I'm going back home."

"But how?" I glance around the room. "Where is this portal? The sink? You cannot fit down a sink, Johnny."

"I can't explain. There's no time. But you gotta promise me something." He grips my hands and stares me in the eyes. How dark his irises are. "Promise me that no matter what I say at the trial, you'll go along with it."

My stomach clenches. "What do you plan to say?"

"Just promise me. You have to. Don't wreck this for me. Please! I'm begging you, man." Johnny's eyes tear up, the whites reddening. His upper lip trembles. His nose starts to run. "Please, Boo."

"But, Johnny, who is Gunboy?" I keep my voice down. "The boy in your nightmares, who *is* he?"

He wipes his nose with the back of his hand.

"You wanna know?" he whispers, even hoarser now. "Gunboy is madness. My madness, your madness, everybody's madness in this f*cking nightmare of a heaven."

"*Our* madness?"

He cradles his pencil box in his lap. He speaks to it, or perhaps to his roach, when he says, "I was sick in the head. Gunboy was the mad me, the crazy me. He's been hunting me for a long time. Even back in America, he was after me."

"But you are not Gunboy anymore, are you?"

"Maybe I am. Maybe I'll always be a little bit mental." He looks at me again, eyes still glistening.

Reginald calls out, "Two minutes!"

"I'll explain everything later, okay? Just promise to back me up at the trial. Don't contradict what I say. And don't tell nobody you're doing this. Not even Thelma and Esther."

I simply stare at him. I do not know what to say.

"Promise me, Boo!" he says louder. "You owe me."

What do I owe this boy, this Gunboy? I do not know, but I nod nonetheless. "I promise," I say.

"Time's up!" Reginald shouts. He strides into the cell and grabs me by the arm. "Come, come," he says, digging his fingernails into my biceps. I do not move, so he wrenches me up, and I cry out in pain.

In a flash, Johnny grabs Thelma's peach pie. He rises and smashes it into the side of Reginald's head. Peach preserves smear across the president's cheek. Piecrust sticks to his $E = mc^2$. A nail file and an aluminum plate fall to his feet.

Reginald lets go of my arm. He backs toward the door, barking, "Guards! Guards!"

"Look, Boo!" Johnny says. "A piebald covered in pie."

"Get out, Oliver!" Reginald orders, wiping his face furiously with his hands. "Wait outside." He points into the hall.

I stay put.

Ringo dashes into the cell and says, "Oh, what'd you do now, Johnny boy?"

"I'm sick to death of this lunacy," Reginald says, picking peach slices off his clothes and flicking them in Johnny's direction. "It has no place in our sweet hereafter."

A second guard appears. Burly. A black crew cut. He walks toward Johnny, puts up his dukes, and punches him square in the nose. Johnny stumbles back and falls to the floor. I try to go to him, but Ringo grabs my arm.

The burly guard jiggles his fist and says, "Ow, that hurt."

Johnny lies motionless on his side, blood dripping from one nostril. Then he reaches out, plucks up a peach slice lying nearby, and plops it into his mouth. "Happy now, j*ckoffs?" he mumbles. "I'm eating."

"WE TOLD THE JAILERS NOT TO ALLOW THE GRADE F THAT PIE," TIM
Lu says, "but did they listen to us? No, as usual, they did not."

"And they suffered the consequences," Tom Lu adds.

"Oh, what a brouhaha!"

"A real hullabaloo!"

The twins are watching us from their reception desk. I am
back in the Gene's lobby, sitting between Esther and Thelma
on a bench. The girls are trying to calm me down. I became
wheezy while recounting what had happened, so Esther passed
me the paper bag she keeps in her sunflower purse to treat my
attacks. Now I am breathing in and out to restore my levels of
carbon dioxide.

I take the bag away. "Rover has helped him find a portal," I
whisper. "He is going home. Or so he claims."

"I don't trust Rover," Esther says. "When we had the chance,
we should have flushed that turd down the toilet."

"Johnny hasn't ate in over a week," Thelma says. "He might
just be hallucinating a portal. The boy ain't himself."

"Well, who the hell is the real *himself*? That's what I wanna
know," Esther replies.

I do not mention my vow to agree with whatever Johnny
says at his trial, which starts in three days. I am unsure about
what my promise may mean. What foolish claims is he planning to make?

The girls and I shuffle out of the Gene, our faces woebe-
gone, our thoughts dark. We climb on our bikes. Esther and

Thelma plan to go back to their dorms in Eleven, but I want to head to Curios to do some work. When I arrive there more than an hour later, a cardboard box awaits me in my office. In it are new curious objects freshly delivered from Two for me to appraise. I am glad for the distraction: it gives me a break from thinking about the madness of the past weeks and the madness that lies ahead.

I open the box and spread the items across my desk. I pick up a spray bottle of a perfume called Tigress. The stopper is designed in fake tiger fur. The bottle is half full, and I spritz some of the amber-colored perfume into the air. It smells like cinnamon.

A windup music box is another of the items. When I open it, instead of a ballerina, there appears an ugly little gnome astride a broken witch's broom. The figurine sits on a spring and wobbles while the music to the children's song "The Wobblin' Goblin" plays. This song is close to my heart because when I was a child, you would sing it to me, Mother. I let the music box play as I examine the other new objects.

There is a paperback book titled *A Glossary of Accounting Terms*, one of the closest things to a dictionary that has been seen in heaven. I flip through the pages but find the book of little interest. After all, townies need not understand the concept of "cash flow statements" and "merit salary adjustments."

There is a half-finished tube of anti-acne cream. I screw off the cap and press out a dab of the stuff. It is flesh-colored and smells of sulfur (No. 16, abbreviated as S).

I am examining a meat tenderizer resembling a small hammer when there is a knock on my open door. I look up to see my boss, Peter Peter.

"Anything of note in the new batch?"

I hold up a box of Lucky Charms cereal. Usually Zig sends us

wholesome cereal like bran flakes and shredded wheat. Though
Peter Peter came to heaven long ago, he has kept up with developments in America, thanks to newbies, whom he regularly
interviews. Hence he knows about anti-acne creams and cereals
containing miniature marshmallows in assorted colors.

"I'm surprised a warehouse worker didn't wolf those down,"
Peter Peter says. Often the edibles do not arrive at our offices
intact.

"It is fortified with eight essential vitamins," I say.

"Is that so?" Peter Peter replies.

I study the ingredients list for a moment, and when I look
up, Peter Peter is still there, smiling sadly.

"Oliver, may I have a word in private?"

I nod. I wonder what he means by "in private." Nobody else
is around. Still, when Peter Peter steps into my office, he shuts
the door behind him. He drags a chair in front of my desk and
fiddles with his necktie, which he wears in a thick Windsor
knot over his T shirt. "I have something to propose to you," he
says, "something I've touched on in our past discussions. You
recall our talk on last-minute edits?"

I nod. Like many other townies, Peter Peter speculates that
a person who died a vile death does not recall all the details. He
may recall the basics. He knows, for example, that he leaped
out a fifth-story window during a fire that engulfed his family's
apartment, but he does not remember the searing pain as his
clothes caught fire, the horrific panic, the sickening plunge, or
the brutal impact with the sidewalk. I use this example because
it is the one Peter Peter used with me. He died in this manner
in the thirties on the Upper East Side of Manhattan.

"You mentioned I may not remember the nitty-gritty of the
shooting at my school," I say. "That certain images, sounds, and
feelings might be forever buried in my brain."

"I never said 'forever.'"

I throw him a questioning look.

"There's a way to recover some of our lost memories, son. I know because I recovered some of mine long ago."

I point the meat tenderizer at him. "So you do remember the sickening plunge and the brutal impact?"

"Regrettably, yes," he says. "Zig does us a favor with last-minute edits. If you die a death like mine, you shouldn't know all the details. That's why I don't often talk about the method for retrieving memories. But, in your case, knowing all the facts might help."

I lean across my desk toward Peter Peter and ask how he recovered his memories.

"I had the help of a specialist decades ago. Somebody who's now an old boy like me."

"Will you introduce me to him?"

Peter Peter swallows, and his Adam's apple seems to get caught in his Windsor-knotted tie. He looks almost pained when he says, "You already know him."

"I do?"

"He's a hypnotist."

49   114.82

In

Indium

THE LAST TIME I SAW CZAR, AT THE SAL PARADISE INFIRMARY, HIS face was so swollen and battered I could not tell what he really looked like, but when I meet him on the evening before Johnny's trial, I realize he looks only slightly like the dead-or-alive poster Johnny drew. True, both boys have big, sharp incisors and ears that stick out, but the Gunboy in the drawing had a broad nose and Czar's nose is slender and crooked. Gunboy's eyebrows were thick and black; Czar's eyebrows are fine and fair.

The day before Johnny's trial commences, Czar and I meet at Curios on the settee beside the display of American coinage, featuring ten Susan B. Anthony dollars, which I have taken out to clean. As he approaches the settee, Czar says, "I hope you don't have a f*cking flashlight on you."

He is making a droll reference to the attack, but fortunately his injuries have healed completely. Not even a remnant of a bruise is visible.

"You're looking well, Czar," I say.

"No thanks to you," he replies as he sits down beside me.

"I am so sorry for the dreadful error that resulted in your infirmary stay," I tell him. "Though I did not wield the flashlight, I am as much to blame as Johnny Henzel. I wish to make amends. Is there anything I can do for you?"

"Well, Petey says you're a smart whippersnapper. So what you can do is find me a real portal."

I think of Johnny and his claim to have found one.

"Time's running out. Find me one before my expiry date."

Czar is also forty-six heaven years old, and hence he will repass in four years' time.

"Well, I can try. Once the trial is over, perhaps I will have more time to devote to new projects."

Czar says he will testify tomorrow. He does not recall the beating—"Your sicko friend knocked me out cold with his first blow"—so he will talk about his injuries, his recovery, his anger.

"I'm mad as hell about the weeks you two goofballs stole from me." He taps his index finger against my sternum. "I'm no spring chicken. I don't have much time left, so I can't afford to be in a coma for almost two f*cking months."

He taps his finger harder and harder to underline the seriousness of his ordeal. In fact, he looks so peeved I begin to fear for my safety. Peter Peter is around the corner in his office, and he said that if Czar becomes too brutish, I should call out. The two old boys, despite their different characters, have been friends since the year of their original passing, when they shared a room in Four. I wonder if Peter Peter appealed to Czar's sense of duty by evoking the parallels between their friendship and mine with Johnny.

"His brutality is mostly an act," Peter Peter assured me. "Charles behaves like a czar because he thinks he gets more respect if he appears intimidating."

Czar hypnotizes in private. He needs absolute silence and no distractions, and that is why Peter Peter is waiting in his office. The hypnotist wears a T-shirt with a sketch of a magician pulling a rabbit out of a top hat. "Let's get this show on the road," he announces. He gets up from the settee and tells me to lie down. He goes over to the light switches and dims the overhead lamps. Then he walks around the room and switches off the individual lamps we shine on our different displays. "For a hypnosis, I like it nice and dark," he says.

I am prepared for some form of ruse. For the so-called hauntings of his, Czar first drew information from his subjects about their former lives so he could invent stories to feed to them while they were hypnotized. But Czar has a very real power, Peter Peter told me. He can help townies recall the final moments of their deaths—in details they do not remember in their afterlife. "Not every detail," Peter Peter warned. "There may still be blank spots, like missing frames in a film reel, but you'll certainly have a fuller picture of your death."

Peter Peter said that Czar keeps this power of his mostly under wraps because it has had tragic consequences. Years ago, a gommer attempted suicide after learning the full details of her rape and death at her uncle's hands. As a result, I promised I would not speak to others about my hypnosis whatever the outcome might be.

"Don't move a muscle, okay?" Czar tells me.

The settee, though worn, is still very padded, so I feel comfortable. I cross my arms and rest them on my chest, but Czar says, "You look like a frigging corpse in a coffin," so I move my arms to my side.

"I want you to recount to me the details of your death," Czar says. "Then once you're under my spell, I'll feed these details back to you gradually like a cook adding oats to boiling water. I need to stimulate the brain slowly so it releases both the remembered memories and the lost memories. If I go too quickly, the scene will play back too fast and there'll be too many holes for you to follow what's going on."

I am unsure whether to believe in this exercise, but out of my desperation to understand the madness that struck Johnny and me, I will give it a try. I describe my final moments in America: the hallway, Jermaine Tucker, Richard Dawkins and Jane Goodall, the periodic table, the countdown to seaborgium.

When I have finished my story, Czar kneels beside the settee. "Breathe deeply through your nose," he tells me. From his pants pocket, he takes out a fake gold chain with a blue bauble attached to its end. The thing looks like the gaudy jewelry sold in gumball machines in America. He tells me it is blue topaz. He swings it above my face, and I follow the bauble with my eyes.

IN HER GRADUATION GOWN AND MORTARBOARD, HELEN KELLER looks down at me from her portrait on the wall. I am standing in front of my locker, No. 106, and turning the dial of my lock—to 7 and then to 25 and then to 34. Around me, I hear the laughter and cries of my fellow students. Their voices say or shout or sing such things as "Can I borrow your lip gloss?" and "Up your nose with a rubber hose!" and "Shake your body down to the ground!" and "Go, Trojans, go!" and "Miss Stephens got herself a Dorothy Hamill do!"

I swing open my locker. Taped to the inside of its door are two magazine pictures, one of evolutionary biologist Richard Dawkins and one of primatologist Jane Goodall. My classmates have mocked me for putting up pictures of my "parents" in my locker.

Also on the inside of my locker door is a copy of the periodic table. I have concocted a game whereby I must try to recite the elements in chronological order whenever I open my locker. I am trying to memorize all 106 of them.

I mumble the elements under my breath. Beside me, Jermaine Tucker fishes a textbook out of the holy mess that is his own locker. I am at No. 78, platinum (Pt), when he cuffs me hard on the back of the head. He is an athletic boy several inches taller than I, so his cuff hurts, but I remind myself I have a high threshold for pain.

"What the hell you doing, Boo?" he says. I ignore his question and continue with my mumbling. I find it best not to make eye contact when a classmate begins harassing me because sometimes a lack of response causes the person to lose interest. My tactic works, and Jermaine Tucker wanders off.

The noises around me, the shouts and guffaws, fade away as I fall back into the world of elements. For the first time, I *do* reach No. 106, seaborgium (Sg), without needing to steal a peek at the periodic table. My second parents, Richard and Jane, are thoroughly pleased and smile from their photographs as though to congratulate me on my feat. I smile back at them.

"Good-bye," I whisper to them, just as I always do before heading off to class. Then I reach for something inside my locker.

Blackness. Silence.

I am now as blind and deaf as Helen Keller herself. I suppose there is nothing more to see or hear in this world. I suppose I am dead. I wait to be reborn.

But these few moments are simply missing frames in my film reel, because an instant later light seeps in, sounds erupt, and I can see again.

What I see is horrific. I am on the floor and a boy is lying within arm's reach. His eyelids flutter, his eyes look without seeing, his face contorts, and his blood seeps from the side of his head and drenches his long brown hair.

Then the darkness swallows me again. But not the silence. A scream fills my head. A scream so bloodcurdling, so nightmarish, it wakes me from my trance.

WHEN I COME TO, THELMA IS BEATING UP CZAR. SHE HAS PUSHED him to the floor and is straddling him. She slaps him in the face with her big, meaty hands. Once, twice, thrice. "What'd you do to him?" she cries. "Tell me, you son of a b*tch!"

Czar flails his arms. "Ouch! Stop! Ouch!" he hollers.

I sit up, groggy, on the settee as Peter Peter runs in, his tie flapping. He hurries over to pull Thelma off Czar.

"You people are all f*cking nuts!" Czar yells as he struggles to get up. His T-shirt is torn at the neck and his hair disheveled. "Why do I try helping you when all I get is bruises and concussions?"

Peter Peter looks dismayed. He brushes the dust off his friend's back as Thelma straightens her kitten T-shirt, which has ridden up her belly.

"I'm a professional hypnotist!" Czar cries. "I deserve respect, but all I get is f*cking abuse!" He swats at the display of ten Susan B. Anthonys, and the dollar coins go flying and then bounce across the floor in a jingle-jangle. How upset I will be if we lose one!

Thelma comes to sit with me on the settee. "Are you okay, Oliver?" She places her fingertips on my elbow as a gesture of concern.

"I feel very curious," I say.

"What the hell were you doing to him?" Thelma says, scowling at Czar. "You some kind of maniac?"

"I ain't the maniac!" Czar snaps, his voice now high-pitched. "You people are the maniacs!"

Peter Peter steps forward. "I'm afraid this is entirely my fault."

Czar says, "I should have known not to get mixed up in this filthy business." He turns on his heel and storms off.

"Charles, wait," Peter Peter calls out. At the corned beef display, Czar turns around and gives Peter Peter the finger.

"No need to be uncivilized," Peter Peter calls out.

"F*ck off and redie!" Czar yells. Then he stomps out of the exhibition hall.

Once Czar is gone, I tell Thelma we were conducting an experiment. I am still dazed, still partly immersed in my horrible lost memory.

"I was worried, honey. You didn't come home this evening, so I biked here to see if you was okay and I found that kook standing over you. I thought he was killing you, 'cause all a sudden you started hollerin'."

"Was I screaming?" It is true my voice sounds hoarse.

"To high heaven," Thelma says.

Peter Peter explains what Czar was doing. He must trust his new girlfriend, because he discloses everything, even his own fiery plunge from his penthouse apartment. Thelma keeps patting her own cheeks as though to revive her circulation. When Peter Peter is finished, she says, "This is dangerous information."

Peter Peter replies, "So dangerous I urge you to keep it secret."

Thelma nods slowly. Then she turns to me. With a mix of dread and excitement, she says, "Tell me what you saw, Oliver."

I tell them I did not see who shot me. "But I must not have died immediately from my wound," I say, almost breathless. "I must have passed out and then come to next to Johnny."

Thelma and Peter Peter give me looks of sympathy. In a way,

these two thirteen-year-olds are my foster parents, not Richard and Jane.

"You saw him?" Peter Peter prods. "You saw Johnny?"

"The last thing I saw," I say, "was the bloody bullet hole in his head."

"Zig in heaven," Thelma whispers, and then she glowers at Peter Peter for having arranged this experiment. "Who was screaming?" she asks me. "Was it you? Or was it Johnny?"

I blink a few times, as if the light in the dim room is still too bright. "I believe it was I," I say. "But I do not believe I was screaming aloud. I believe I was screaming in my head."

Mother. I want my real mother. I want you. And, Father, where are you? I want you too. I think I may break my rule of never crying. But I do not. I sit silently on the settee and stare at a dollar coin that rolled under our display of dead telephones that will never ring.

52	127.60
Te	
Tellurium	

I TELL THELMA I WILL WORK INTO THE WEE HOURS BECAUSE MY insomnia will surely keep me up tonight. I do not tell her I have not slept in days. Still, she is not pleased. "You need your rest," she scolds, waving her hands about. "The trial starts tomorrow. You need to be fresh." I lie that I will sleep on the couch in my office, and she finally caves in. Before she leaves, she wraps her arms around herself and squeezes. This is our code: when she hugs herself this way, she means she is hugging me. Peter Peter tells me not to work too hard. "Don't kill yourself, son," he says, and then looks away embarrassed because his wording is ill-chosen.

"Rest in peace," they both tell me as they are leaving.

I decide to spend the night here because I need to talk to Zig. I feel closer to him at Curios, probably because I am surrounded by the unusual objects he sends our way. The shelves lining my office walls are filled with these objects. A bottle of white wine from the Napa Valley, a cash register, a jumbo box of diapers, a biography of American crooner Barry Manilow, a slender electric razor used to trim nostril hairs. And on and on and on.

Some objects are obvious mistakes, things Zig sent us accidentally. Falling into this category are diapers (newborns here are already toilet-trained, ha-ha) and nostril-hair trimmers (boys here have little facial hair, certainly no protruding nostril hairs).

But other items may not be mistakes. Two weeks ago, for

instance, our heaven received its first photocopier, a clunky, stove-size machine now shoved into a corner of my office near the door. Like all electrical devices, it works without being plugged in. I suppose—and Peter Peter tends to agree—that the photocopier is a test. Zig wishes to see how we will make use of this new contraption, just as, a year ago, he sent us our first microwave oven and, decades ago, he sent us our first washing machine.

Will we use the photocopier wisely? Will we, say, copy the books, stories, and plays we write? Will we distribute these works of fiction throughout Town for others to enjoy? If so, Zig may send us other photocopiers. Or will we use the device recklessly, maybe to copy dead-or-alive posters of a Gunboy we wish to put to death?

In other words, we may be his guinea pigs. My guinea-pig theory is what I wish to discuss with him tonight. I sit at my desk and turn the crank on my music box. The little figurine wiggles on his broom as the box tinkles out its playful tune about the pitiful goblin who trades in his broken broom for an airplane.

I identify with this goblin tonight. Boo, too, is wobbly. My hand trembles as I turn the crank. My voice is shaky as I speak aloud. "You are watching, aren't you?" I say, looking at my beat-up couch as though our old god is lounging there like an old dog. I must say I feel silly—I have never spoken to Zig like this. "You sent us a photocopier to see what we would do with it," I say. "And you sent us a Gunboy to see what we would do with him."

I am admitting aloud to Zig that Johnny may have killed someone (killed *me*, I should say). Maybe I am the last person involved to come to this conclusion. I came to it slowly because, as a junior scientist, I do not jump to conclusions.

"Johnny Henzel is a curious object, but he is no mistake," I go on. "You fixed him as best you could. You tinkered with his faulty parts and erased his painful memories so he can cope in his afterlife. And now you want to see how townies react to this boy you dropped into their world."

The god sprawled on the couch stays invisible.

"Is my theory right?"

No answer.

"Speak up!"

My music box winds down. The goblin stops wobbling.

"Johnny is a test case. If we all pass your test, if we all show mercy and compassion to this boy you fixed, maybe one day you will send us more boys like him."

I pick up my music box and turn the crank again.

"Townies all say heaven is a second chance. Why shouldn't we give Johnny his?"

No more music comes out of the music box. I keep cranking but for naught. Darn it. Is the goblin already broken? When I shake the box, I hear something rolling around beneath the platform that the goblin wobbles on. Batteries? No, that makes no sense: music boxes run on cranks, and batteries are not needed in heaven. I take my fake-tortoiseshell letter opener and wedge it under the edge of the platform. With a little elbow grease on my part, the platform springs up.

I peek inside the box.

What the dickens?!

I drop the music box on my desk and push back my chair so fast it almost overturns. I stand there flabbergasted for a second or two before throwing an angry eye at the couch.

"What foul tricks are you playing, you old dog?"

Inside the goblin's music box, lying side by side, are two bullets.

AT SEVEN O'CLOCK IN THE MORNING, THELMA AND ESTHER ARRIVE
at Curios so we can bike to the Gene together to attend Johnny's
trial. When they knock on my office door, I do not immediately
respond. They push open the door and find me lying on the
floor in my boxers and an undershirt. I am in an insomniac stupor. My fifth straight night without sleep. I lift a hand weakly
to wave to the girls.

I am not strong. Why did Johnny ever think differently?

The girls are dressed spiffily in argyle kilts sewn by Esther.
Esther has her hair in a tight bun; Thelma has on her usual
beads. When they see the state I am in—unshowered, blurry-
eyed, hair on end—they are fretful.

"Oh, honey, you ain't hunky-dory!" Thelma pulls me up and
brings me to the couch to sit.

"You look like death warmed over," Esther tells me as she
pinches my cheeks to add some color. "We can't have the jurors
pitying you. They'll hand Johnny his butt on a platter."

"What's this?!" Thelma yells because she notices cuts on my
forearms. During the night, in my despair, I struck myself again
and again with the meat tenderizer.

"A scab-healing experiment," I lie.

"Damn it, Boo!" Esther cries. "Pull yourself together, man."

Peter Peter arrives in my office to wish me luck at the trial.
When my boss hears Esther complaining that I look ghostly,
he takes the anti-acne cream from my desk and tells her to dab
some on. "It's flesh-colored," he says.

Thelma says, "It ain't my flesh color, honey."

It is not mine either. It is orangey beige. Still, Esther spreads a thin layer across my cheeks and forehead. It smells of sulfur, which, long ago, was known as brimstone. Brimstone does not bode well for the trial, but I do not tell the others this because they seem pleased now with the color of my complexion.

Peter Peter fetches a long-sleeved T-shirt from his office. It is too big for me, but at least it is not wrinkled. As I slide my scabby arms into it, he loosens his necktie and then slips it around my neck. Thelma drags a comb through my flyaway hair.

Esther rummages in her purse and pulls out an apple as well as a peanut-butter-and-jam sandwich wrapped in plastic. "Eat," she tells me. The apple is crisp and tart and gives me a boost. When I finish my breakfast, the girls and I prepare to leave for the jail. Peter Peter says he will close Curios today and come along with us, but I try to dissuade him. I have grown fond of our museum: it gives me a purpose in heaven other than helping Johnny. It should not be shut down, but Peter Peter cannot be deterred, and so we all head downstairs. Esther stuffs her sunflower purse into the basket of her bicycle. Thelma suggests biking slowly so I do not sweat my makeup off.

"I assure you I rarely expire," I say.

I mean, of course, "perspire." A Freudian slip due to my fatigue and general malaise.

We ride our bicycles into the street. Traffic is heavy today despite the early hour. The sky is blanketed with Johnny's holy mackerel clouds. Did Zig whip up these clouds as a good omen? Do I even believe in signs from our goddamn god?

Were the two bullets an offering from him? Well, I do not need such an offering. I hid the bullets at the back of my desk drawer in an empty eyeglasses case. I refuse to check if the bullets fit in the little revolver displayed in Curios. Go to hell, Zig! I do not need your little games!

We cycle for a good hour and a half. When we approach the Gene, we are surprised to see the number of townies the trial is attracting. Hundreds of people are crowded on the prison's front lawn. Dozens of protesters wield picket signs. Gommers, I guess. I try to avoid reading their placards, but I glimpse one that reads, PUT HIM OUT OF OUR MISERY.

While parking my bicycle, I notice a makeshift stage with a spray-painted banner that reads, LOTTERY TICKETS. Tim and Tom Lu climb onto the stage. One of them is carrying a bass drum, which he sets down. They both pick up bullhorns that had been lying on the stage floor.

"Wow, Tim," Tom says into his bullhorn, "the Grade F is more popular than Jesus Christ."

"Right you are, Tom. That's why we're holding a raffle to assign the two hundred seats available in the Gene's auditorium."

"Can we pack everybody in?"

"I guesstimate there are five hundred people here, so I'd say, nope, they won't all get a seat. Folks have to take a number from our assistants wandering through the crowd. Then we'll draw numbers out of this here bass drum to see who gets in."

"Oh, what fun!"

"Now, Tom, don't be disrespectful. This is a murder trial, after all. It's serious business. It's not a play. It's not *The Teahouse of the August Moon*."

"What about official witnesses and victims, Tim? Do they need a lottery number?"

"Don't be silly, Tom. Of course not. They have the best seats in the house. Front row, center. To avoid the crowd, witnesses and victims should enter the Gene by the side door."

Peter Peter says he will go fetch a number. He wishes me luck and pats himself on the shoulder.

As Thelma, Esther, and I weave through the crowd, I notice that the jail looks even more dismal than usual, as though another layer of soot settled on it overnight. And the lawn we cross is so infested with weeds that we decapitate dandelions with almost every step we take. I must invent a natural pesticide (maybe using cayenne pepper) to keep the dandelion population at bay.

A long-haired boy with an acoustic guitar strapped to his back ambles up. "Hey, aren't you Boo?"

I nod uneasily.

The hippie's face lights up. "How about an autograph?"

"Bug off," Esther spits.

"I'm writing a song about you and Johnny, Boo. It's called 'The Gun and the Damage Done.'"

"We're in a hurry," Thelma tells the hippie.

"Break a leg, my man," the hippie says.

An albino girl, with normal eyesight restored by Zig, points at me. "I love you, Boo!" she squeals.

My bodyguards, Thelma and Esther, walk on either side of me. Thelma tells me my story has managed to travel from dorm to dorm across Town.

"But like all stories that spread around heaven," Esther says, "it's been perverted in the telling."

When we reach the side door of the prison, a girl jailer in a purple armband is there to greet us. She checks our names off her list of witnesses and then leads us down a hallway to a waiting room where another jailer, the big-nosed Ringo again, stands watch over peanut girl Sandy Goldberg and portal seeker Benny Baggarly.

Benny barely looks up, but Sandy waves and says, "Hello,

Thelma. Hello, Boo." She is still wearing tight braids, which stick straight out from both sides of her head as though she uses pipe cleaners as a support system. "Gosh, I never knew my afterlife would be so busy," she says. "With badminton finals and this trial, I'm, like, super booked. If you can believe it, I'm even more popular here than I was back home!"

We take our seats. Picture a dentist's waiting room, Mother and Father, and you will imagine this space. It is even painted the mint green of toothpaste found in America.

Esther whispers to me, "I have another peanut butter sandwich in my purse. Should I slip it to the nutter?"

"Food allergies do not exist in heaven," I say. "Nobody dies here of anaphylactic shock."

Unlike Esther and me, Thelma is good at small talk, so she asks Sandy about her badminton tournaments. While Sandy talks about vertical jump smashes and sliced drop shots, another witness is brought to the room. It is Albert Schmidt, the Deborah's baby-faced manager, whom we met on the day Willa Blake threw herself off the roof of the asylum. Because he is tiny and wears a red bow tie and a straw hat, he reminds me of the little monkeys that played cymbals on street corners in the olden days.

Thelma interrupts Sandy's description of her trademark shot, a round-the-head forehand overhead. "What are *you* doing here?" she asks Albert.

"To tell you the truth, I'm not sure," Albert tells us. "The warden sent word she wanted me to come."

"Maybe to talk about sadness and confusion," I suggest.

Just then, Charles "Czar" Lindblom shows up, his hair oiled back and his jeans ironed with a crease.

"Try not to beat me into a coma, okay?" he says to Thelma and me.

"I should feel sorry for that fella," Thelma whispers to me. "But instead I want to slap him upside his head."

Czar sits down beside Benny Baggarly. I wonder if Benny harbors ill will toward Czar with the hauntings exposed as the hoax of a hypnotist. I guess not, since Benny offers him a comic book he has brought along.

For the most part, we sit in silence. I fret about Johnny. Is he waiting in the auditorium where the trial will take place? Is he nervous about the outcome? Will he be happy to see the girls and me?

"When will this Punch and Judy show get started?" Esther asks Ringo, who stands in the doorway shifting his weight from leg to leg.

"Hold your horses, love," he replies.

Esther says, "*Love?!* Who are you calling love? I'm not your love, mister!"

Ringo gives her an amused look. "Don't be such a twat," he says.

"*Twat?!*" Esther says. "How'd you like a kick in the nuts?"

"Oh, sod off," Ringo replies.

"Settle down now," Thelma tells Esther.

We end up waiting another hour, all of us growing more and more fidgety. Finally, another jailer tells Ringo to escort us to the trial. We march down several corridors and then enter the auditorium, which looks disturbingly like all the other theaters in heaven, theaters where we are entertained by plays, concerts, and dances put on by townies. This trial, I understand, is another kind of entertainment for the audience that has come today. Townies with winning raffle tickets—all two hundred of them—are already seated when the other witnesses and I are led to the front row.

Thelma spots Peter Peter and waves.

"Rest in peace, Boo!" somebody calls out, and Ringo cries, "No shouting! Shouters will be thrown out!"

When we move to our seats, Czar turns to look at the audience. He spreads his arms wide and smiles broadly. I would not be surprised if he took a bow. Esther kicks him in the shin. "Sorry," she mutters, though I suspect she is anything but.

There are seven empty flip-up seats in the front row. I sit in the middle, with Esther and Thelma on either side. Beside Esther are Czar and Benny. Beside Thelma are Sandy and Albert. Once we are all seated, the audience claps as though we are members of an orchestra tuning up to perform a concert.

In the center of the stage is a heavy padded armchair that looks less threadbare than most of the furniture in heaven. A spotlight is trained on the chair, which is covered in red fabric, a poor color choice because it evokes blood.

Desk chairs are set in a row on both sides of the stage. They will accommodate the warden and the thirteen jurors (one townie chosen randomly from each of the zones). Once we witnesses are seated, they march out from the wings and take their seats behind the desks. The warden is wearing her cashmere-like sweater and her badge (a good sign). As the house lights dim, she nods into the wings, and council president Reginald Washington and jailer Ringo lead Johnny Henzel onto the stage. Members of the audience gasp, though there is nothing unusual about Johnny. He is not dressed in the regular prison garb of orange shorts and an orange T-shirt, but instead in clean jeans and a plain white T-shirt. He looks healthier than the last time I saw him. Indeed, his appearance is heartening, apart from the handcuffs around his wrists.

A few people in the audience hiss as Ringo escorts my friend to the hot seat, sits him down, and then unlocks his handcuffs. I am sitting right in front of Johnny, though several yards away.

His eyes blink because the spotlight is on him. With the house lights off, he may not be able to see much of the audience. I wave to him, and I think I catch his eye, but then he looks away. He stares straight up at the spotlight like a boy blinding himself during an eclipse by looking into the sun.

Reginald stands at the front left side of the stage. He sets his notes on a podium and introduces himself by speaking into the podium microphone. "Reginald Washington, president of the do-good council of Eleven for eight years running," he says. "I hope to win a third term, so if any of you good people are from Eleven, remember this face in next spring's election." He gives the audience a smile that looks misleadingly sweet.

Reginald says we are here today for a first in the history of our heaven, a trial at which an accused will be judged for crimes committed not only in the afterlife but also down in America. When he says "down in America," he glances at me, but I look away. I look at Johnny, who is still staring upward at the humming spotlights.

I feel almost jet-lagged from lack of sleep. Esther and Thelma pat their own knees, which means they are patting mine. Esther takes my CO_2 bag from her sunflower purse. "Just in case," she says, handing it over.

I fold and unfold the bag as Reginald explains the details of the accusations against Johnny. He starts with Johnny's rebirth and quotes Thelma as saying the newborn was bewildered and in tears. "The accused told the rebirthing nurse he'd been shot in the head at his junior high and endured five weeks in a coma before succumbing to his injuries."

Reginald adds that Thelma paired him with another newbie killed in the same shooting. "That boy, Oliver Dalrymple, was unaware of the real cause of his death."

Somebody in the audience shouts, "Boo!"

"No bloody shouting!" Ringo yells into a bullhorn from where he is stationed at the side of the stage.

I watch Johnny, but he does not appear to be listening to Reginald. He looks innocent, as he did on the day during the tornado drill in Hoffman Estates—when everyone else was scared and excited and he sat quietly under his desk and calmly asked to draw me.

Reginald continues presenting what he calls "the facts." He says he mulled over whether it was wise and safe to send our little group on a journey to track down "the mysterious Gunboy." "Though I had misgivings, former council member Thelma Rudd pleaded with me to assist this boy in distress who was not adapting well to his new habitat."

"Baloney," mutters Thelma. She brought along a Japanese hand fan and is waving it in front of her face. "Reginald suggested the road trip himself."

Reginald recounts our trip, including Johnny's disappearance after we witnessed what Reginald calls "an apparent suicide" at the Deborah Blau Infirmary. He describes the "unprovoked and violent attack" on Charles Lindblom and the "shocking and disturbing revelations" of Sandy Goldberg.

From her seat, Sandy pipes up: "All I remember, everybody, is that there was just two guys killed. A crazy one and a weird one. That's basically all I got to say."

Reginald stops his talk and smiles uneasily at Sandy. "Thank you, Ms. Goldberg," he says. "But no further interruptions, please." He goes on to mention that the do-good council from Eleven ordered our recapture. "There was an urgent need not only to protect townies from this dangerous boy but also to separate the victim, Oliver Dalrymple, from the killer who cut short his first life."

"Boo!" a girl calls out.

"Put a sock in it!" Ringo shouts.

Reginald continues: "I interviewed John Henzel several times in his jail cell about the wicked crimes of which he stands accused. It is time I share with you what I learned, particularly in recent days. Mr. Henzel, are you ready to tell us your story?"

Johnny stops gazing at the rafters. He lowers his eyes till they are level with the audience. Ringo crosses the stage and hands him a microphone. Johnny turns it on. A squeal rips through the hall, and I jump in my seat. It takes me a moment to realize the noise is from the microphone, not from Johnny.

When the squeal dies, Johnny holds the microphone to his mouth. "I am Gunboy," he says.

From behind me, somebody whispers, "Kill him, kill him."

"You're confessing to your crimes?" Reginald asks.

I can barely breathe.

"Yeah," Johnny says with conviction.

"When did you discover you were the so-called Gunboy?"

"I've always known. Even back in America I knew."

"You knew down below."

"Yeah."

"How?"

"Somebody told me every day of my life."

"Who was that somebody?"

"Zig."

A sharp intake of breath from the audience.

"You mean you talk to Zig?" Reginald feigns surprise, though I can tell this exchange was planned. It almost seems as if we are watching a play in which the lines have been memorized.

"I've always talked to him. He tells me to do things."

"What kind of things?"

"Bad things. Real bad things."

Esther whispers to me, "A crock of sh*t." However, there is a tinge of doubt in her voice.

"Does he tell you to kill people?"

"He orders me to. He talks to me through dogs and roaches."

Grumblings in the audience. A boy hollers, "Throw the b*stard off the roof!"

Ringo yells back, "You're banished!"

There is a pause as the house lights go up. I turn in my seat and see two jailers shuffle through the audience toward one of the boys from the gommer meeting I attended. It is the boy whose killer threw him off a bridge. The jailers pull him from his seat and drag him from the hall. *Kill him! Kill him!* the gommer yells, fist-punching the air.

Through his bullhorn, Ringo says, "Any of you other twats want out?"

I glance at Johnny. He is staring at me. He does not speak into the microphone, but I am close enough to read his lips when he mouths the words "I want out."

The lights dim again. Reginald says, "Did Zig tell you to murder Mr. Dalrymple at your school in America?"

My holey heart twinges in my chest.

Johnny swallows loudly. His gulp sounds in the mike.

"Yes," he whispers.

"Why target Mr. Dalrymple?"

Johnny is barely audible now. "Boo was in the wrong place," he mutters. "He was an angel on Earth. He didn't belong there."

"An angel on Earth? What do you mean?"

Johnny speaks almost tenderly now. "Boo was strong and smart and pure," he says. "Too perfect for America. He belonged *here*. Zig said so."

I am feeling weak, stupid, tainted. Why is he making up these ludicrous claims? My breathing is shallow, but I cannot even raise my CO_2 bag to my face. I narrow my eyes at Johnny, but he avoids my gaze.

Thelma tut-tuts. Esther whispers, "I'll be d*mned."

"Zig spoke through your dog, a basset hound?"

"Yeah."

Giggles and hoots from the audience as people picture a talking basset hound with floppy ears and stringy drool.

"So you stole your father's gun. You brought it to school and you killed Mr. Dalrymple and terrorized your classmates."

"I did," Johnny says.

"And you shot yourself in the head because you were also an angel on Earth."

"No, I was a monster!" His voice is suddenly angry. He slaps the arm of his chair. "I'm still a monster. I was supposed to go to hell. That was the deal. Zig said I'd be sent to hell."

"So why did you end up here?"

"Zig's a f*cking fraud!" he shouts into the rafters. "A two-faced liar who sent me to heaven instead!"

Nobody is laughing or hooting anymore. Nobody makes a peep. The audience is awestruck.

"Why do you think Zig lied to you?"

"Zig wants me to kill people here too. I'm his assassin, man. I'm his Gunboy. He talked to me through a roach."

Reginald explains to us that Johnny found a roach at a dormitory in Ten and that the insect has since gone missing.

"What did Zig the roach tell you to do in heaven?"

"To weed out kids who don't belong here."

Hogwash, I think to myself.

Thelma whispers, "What's going on in that boy's head?"

"And whom did Zig tell you to murder here?" Reginald asks Johnny, who glances down at us witnesses before him. His eyes home in on Czar.

"Zig said the hypnotist was a f*cking fraud and didn't deserve an afterlife."

I glance at Czar, who looks dumbfounded and scared, as though he believes Zig did in fact order his death.

"Luckily, Mr. Lindblom survived your beastly attack. But another poor soul wasn't as fortunate, isn't that right?"

Johnny nods.

"You managed to end a townie's afterlife, didn't you, Mr. Henzel?"

"Yeah, I did," Johnny mutters.

"Who?"

I am thoroughly confused at this point.

"Some loony girl named Willa who didn't belong here either. I pushed her off the roof of the Deborah."

A roar goes up from the audience, a roar so loud it drowns out Ringo's shouts into his bullhorn. Somebody behind me shrills, "Stop him before he kills again!" A girl runs down the center aisle grasping what looks like a penknife, but a jailer tackles her to the floor. Beside me, Thelma lets out a yelp. Something has just glanced off her head and is rolling across the stage. It is a rotten apple! A volley of apples follows, thumping and splattering against the stage. Reginald darts into the wings, and many of the jurors scramble out of their seats and follow.

Throughout the mayhem, Johnny sits in his red velvet seat and stares up at the lights above. He is mumbling to himself. He is pretending, I believe, to converse with Zig.

54	131.29

Xe

Xenon

WE WITNESSES HAVE BEEN ESCORTED BACK TO OUR WAITING room because a time-out was called in the trial. Thelma, though, is off in the restroom with Sandy, who offered to scrub the apple gook out of her cornrows with a handkerchief.

Esther is arguing with Ringo, who wants us to sit and wait in silence. Esther wants to question Albert Schmidt, the asylum manager, who is waving Thelma's hand fan in front of his face and muttering, "Dear me."

"No way did Johnny push Willa," Esther shouts at Ringo. "I saw that chick jump. She was bonkers, wasn't she, Albert? She was always threatening to kill herself. She was completely out of her mind!"

"Dear me," Albert repeats.

"For a little person, you sure got a big f*cking mouth," Ringo says to Esther, his arms crossed over his chest.

Esther goes almost as purple as a do-good armband. "I'm reporting you, assh*le. I'll get you fired."

"Yeah, get me sacked. You'll be doing me a favor. I'm tired of this bloody job anyway. I should be a tailor rather than a jailer. Much less headache."

I tell Esther to come sit with me. "It's not worth getting riled," I say, even though I am riled myself and feel sick to my stomach.

"Oh, Esther," I whisper, my voice cracking as though I am finally going through puberty. "Johnny wants to redie."

"What are you talking about?" she says, but by her anxious look, I can tell she knows exactly what I am talking about.

"He wants the redeath penalty."

Redeath, I realize, may be the portal he thinks he has found.

Esther shakes her head. "What kind of game is that imbecile playing? He's so calm and collected even though he's saying the craziest things. It's like he wants to appear sane so that he seems even more dangerous."

"Sane?" Czar scoffs. "As sane as Jack the Ripper."

Esther shoots back, "Too bad you aren't still in a coma."

"For shame!" Benny Baggarly says. "Czar almost redied."

"Dear me!" Albert Schmidt repeats, waving his fan frantically. "A patient was murdered on my watch. How will I ever forgive myself?"

Ringo cries, "*I'll* murder somebody if you all don't shut the f*ck up!"

55	132.91
Cs	
Cesium	

I BELIEVE THAT JOHNNY, DESPITE HIS CLAIMS, HAS NO CLEAR REC-
ollection of the broken boy he used to be. Zig edited Johnny's
memories, which is why he has trouble recalling the last months
of his time in America. The Gunboy he sees in his nightmares
is his madness, yes, but this insanity no longer swallows him
whole as it eventually did in his former life. Perhaps, though,
it still nips at his heels from time to time here in heaven and
makes him claim, for instance, that he pushed a sadcon from
a rooftop.

We are all back in the auditorium, and Reginald is wrapping
up his interrogation. "I have one final question for you, Mr.
Henzel," he says, putting down his notes and resting his hands
on the podium. He does not look at Johnny when he asks this
question. He looks instead at the audience.

"What do you consider a just punishment for the crimes
you're pleading guilty to?"

I expect members of the audience, gommers especially, to
cry out the penalty they deem fitting, but nobody says a word.
We all hold our breath. Even the humming from the spotlights
overhead seems to cease.

Johnny lifts his microphone to his lips. He looks my way. He
touches a finger to his eyelid and then reaches out his hand as
if to touch me too.

"An eye for an eye," he says.

"Which means?" Reginald asks.

His eyes still on me, Johnny says, "A tooth for a tooth."

I shake my head and mouth the word "No."

"Damn it," says Esther.

"Heaven help us," says Thelma.

"Justice!" cry the gommers. *"Justice! Justice!"*

"You're requesting the redeath penalty?" Reginald asks.

"I am," says Johnny.

"Yes, yes!" cry the gommers.

"Well, the jurors will certainly take your request into consideration," Reginald says.

Thelma turns to me, her face stricken. "They'll never agree to it. Nobody here has ever been put to redeath."

"Insanity," Esther whispers. "Pure insanity."

Reginald says he has heard enough. "I have no need to hear from any of the witnesses because the accused admits his guilt." He shuffles his notes and then takes a seat.

The warden comes to the podium to address the jurors. "There is still one person," she says, "whom I believe you need to hear from." She looks over at me.

"Boo! Boo!" the audience chants. "Boo! Boo!"

Ringo has given up scolding the crowd. He actually puts his bullhorn to his lips and says, "Boo! Boo!"

"Mr. Dalrymple, would you come to the stage?"

For a second, I am frozen in my seat.

"Go, honey," Thelma says. "Go save your friend from himself."

I rise and shuffle past the other witnesses. Czar looks peeved that he will not be addressing the crowd.

On the side of the stage, I climb the few steps to where the podium is positioned. Meanwhile, two jailers carry out another armchair, a baby blue one, and set it down about a yard from Johnny's chair.

The warden smiles at me, but her forehead has worry lines

that look bizarre on a thirteen-year-old who never ages. She motions to the baby blue chair.

When I draw close, Johnny says, "Hey, Boo," nonchalantly, as though I just ran into him at the school cafeteria.

"Hello, Johnny," I say.

As I sit down in the witness's armchair, a jailer passes me a microphone.

At the podium, Lydia says, "Mr. Dalrymple, I realize you feel sympathy for the accused. Why show him mercy when he showed none to you?"

I look toward the audience. Because of the spotlights, I cannot see terribly well, but I can make out Thelma and Esther. Thelma's cheeks puff out as though she is holding her breath. Esther clutches her sunflower purse. She nods at me.

I turn to Johnny, who stares at me expectantly. His lips utter three words so softly that only I can hear. "Let me go," he says.

I look away. Out in the dark theater, townies await my answer. "Is this horrid boy worth saving?" these people seem to ask. I want to explain that the boy sitting beside me is not a monster. His madness is the monster. I try to speak, but again Johnny mutters under his breath: "Let me go, Boo. You promised."

I shiver. It is as though heaven's usual temperature has just dropped twenty degrees. I try to speak but find I cannot. I open the CO_2 bag in my lap. It is ripped along its creases from my incessant folding and unfolding.

"Mr. Dalrymple, are you okay?" says Lydia Finkle in her fake cashmere.

I nod. I close my eyes. I am bone-weary.

Let me go. Let me go. Let me go.

I picture you, Father and Mother, in your living room. You are building a shelf on the wall. It will be the stage on which my urn will stand. You do not want to let me go. In any case, do we ever really let anyone go? Even those who are no longer with us are still with us.

I must have muttered something aloud because Lydia Finkle says, "Excuse me, Mr. Dalrymple, but we can't hear you. Could you speak into the mike?"

I blink open my eyes. I lift the microphone to my lips and whisper, "Oh, my goodness."

Then it starts. For a second, when I feel the wetness on my cheeks, I think I am bleeding. My hand drops the microphone, and I swat at my cheeks.

Tears.

I am shocked. I emit a groan.

The groan gives way to a sob.

I shut my eyes again. I see Johnny and me, not as we are now, sitting in judgment in front of two hundred people, but as we were then, lying on the floor of Helen Keller. One boy with a hole in his torso, one boy with a hole in his head. Two blood brothers with their blood leaking from their bodies, the rivulets coming together like fingers interlacing.

I see the ghastly wounds, the pooling blood, the terrible sorrow.

I start weeping so violently that I choke on my tears. I lean forward, drop my CO_2 bag. My head spins. I keel over onto the floor.

Blackness. A few missing frames in a film reel.

I come to. I turn over and look up into the rafters and spot-lights. My vision is fuzzy. I blink away tears. Johnny is kneeling beside me, his hands resting lightly on my neck. "I'd never hurt you," he whispers.

"Stop him! Stop that monster!" one of the girl jurors screams. I glance sideways. Ringo is running toward us. He hooks an arm around Johnny's neck and jerks him away from me. More jailers emerge from the wings. They descend on Johnny and carry him off, one jailer with his hands under Johnny's armpits, one jailer grasping his feet.

Into her microphone, Lydia Finkle says, "Mr. Dalrymple, are you all right?"

I sit up as Thelma and Esther rush up the steps to the stage. They hurry over to me. Peter Peter also appears.

Esther kneels beside me. She is wide-eyed, both astonished and vexed. "That idiot!" she cries. "What the hell's he doing? He had his hands around your neck! Was he pretending to strangle you?"

I reach up and touch my neck. It feels fine.

Johnny starts yelling from the wings. *"Booooo! Booooo!"* he shouts in the same critical tone an audience uses when a performance is not to its liking. When he is dragged far enough away that I can no longer hear his voice, I pick up the microphone off the stage floor and hold it to my lips. "Everything Johnny said," I say, "is true."

58 140.12

Ce

Cerium

I CRY ALL THE TIME NOW. I ORDER A STIR-FRY IN THE CAFETERIA and tears dribble down my face ("I'm very sensitive to onions," I lie to the waitress). At Curios, tears fall on my typewriter keys as I type up a notice about our sea monkeys, which are repassing one by one. When I read the novel *Tarzan of the Apes*, I weep when Lord and Lady Greystoke are killed. At this point, I would blubber if, during a trying investigation, Nancy Drew broke a fingernail.

My nickname may soon be Boo Hoo (ha-ha).

I used to pride myself on my independence. In America, I could spend days speaking to no one but you, Mother and Father. I had my morning constitutionals. I had my documentaries on PBS television. I had my books. I had my visits to the library, a place where spending time in one's head is highly valued.

I am still independent, but also lonely—a new feeling for me. I spend plenty of time by myself in my office, where I play the Wobblin' Goblin music box, which is working again. I identify with that poor creature up in the sky, almost falling but somehow managing to stay afloat.

Thelma, Esther, and Peter Peter believe that my mind was muddled after I fainted onstage. That is why, they reason, I corroborated Johnny's version of events. "You didn't know what you were saying, did you, Boo?" Esther asks. "I was confused," I tell her. "Sad and confused." She seems to believe me—or perhaps only pretends and actually wonders whether I am seeking some sort of revenge.

Thelma and Peter Peter worry about me. Peter Peter invites me on father-son outings. Last week, he taught me to catch a football. Thelma came along because her throwing arm is even better than his. The two of them have been seeing a lot of each other. They often exchange gifts. Yesterday, Thelma made him a loaf of zucchini bread, and Peter Peter gave her a half-ounce sample from our bottle of Tigress perfume.

As for Johnny, I have not seen him. Until the do-good council decides on his sentence, I am not allowed to visit. Nonetheless, I go to the jail every day in case a decision is reached.

Tim Lu: "The Grade F is still awaiting his sentence."

Tom Lu: "So no visitors today."

Tim Lu: "When will the pathetic victim get on with his afterlife?"

The gommers still demonstrate outside the Gene, clamoring for the redeath penalty. The method they favor is especially barbaric: a stoning.

I was subject to a kind of stoning, Mother and Father. On the first day of eighth grade, three days before my passing, I arrived home with a bloody nose because Kevin Stein, Nelson Bliss, and Henry Axworthy had whipped rocks at me in the field behind our school. "I was away all summer," Kevin cried, "and boy oh boy did I miss torturing you, Boo," a remark that drew much guffawing from his friends.

Father, you wet a washcloth with warm water and gently wiped away my blood. You said, "Age thirteen was the most dangerous year of my life, son."

My dear gentle father, you, too, had attracted the wrath of bullies.

"But you'll grow up, Oliver," you said. "You'll leave eighth grade far behind."

"Father," I say aloud now, alone in my room, "I'm stuck at age thirteen. I'm stuck here for a frigging lifetime."

59	140.91
Pr	
Praseodymium	

ONE MORNING TWO WEEKS AFTER THE TRIAL, I RISE AT DAWN, SLIP on my cutoff jeans and my peace T-shirt (a decal of a hand making the peace sign), and bicycle all the way to the Gene. As I ride up to the jail, Tim and Tom Lu are on the front steps unrolling a scroll. They tack it to the door and then scurry inside when they see me coming up the driveway.

The notice on the door reads as follows:

IN THE MATTER OF JOHN HENZEL
After due consideration, the thirteen members
of the jury assigned to hear the trial of John
Henzel, reborn on October 12, 1979, and
formerly residing in the GUT district of Eleven,
have reached a unanimous decision in the
sentencing of the prisoner found guilty of
murder and attempted murder. In a manner and
on a date to be revealed in the coming days,
Mr. Henzel will hereby be put to
REDEATH.

I rip down the notice and tear it up. As I fling the bits of paper onto the stairs of the Gene, the front door opens and Tim and Tom Lu step back out.

"Despite that T-shirt of his, the victim sure doesn't look very peaceful," Tim says. He has a second scroll in his hands.

"No, I'd say he looks unhinged," Tom replies.

"I'd go so far as to say 'demented,'" Tim adds.

They stare at me as unblinking as cats. I scowl back.

"Luckily, we made several copies of our communiqué," Tim says, and tacks a second notice to the door.

A few days later, it is also announced that the jury has given its consent to the stoning, which will be held within a week. Technically, however, the stoning will be a "bricking" because, in Town, bricks are easier to come by than large stones. Townies remove loose ones from the exterior walls of schools and dorms, and the holes grow over with new bricks in the same manner that a broken window remakes itself. The bricking being organized is a horrific game of murderball. It will occur on the basketball court of the Marcy, the gymnasium where Johnny and I holed up while on the lam. The brickers will stand on the overhead running track while Johnny kneels handcuffed and ankle-cuffed in the center circle of the basketball court. When the clock strikes midnight, they will all launch their bricks at Johnny. They will keep bashing him with bricks till he is crushed, till he is redead.

The execution is set up in such a way that no one person is the executioner and no one person shoulders the blame. Spread the responsibility among enough people and no one person need feel too guilty. "If I hadn't thrown a brick, he'd have redied anyway," each bricker can claim.

In a murder mystery, the most important piece of evidence is the dead body. Yet, in this killing, there will be no body. Traces of the crime will vanish as Johnny's corpse repasses. Even his spilled blood will disappear into thin air. All that will remain will be a vile quarry of thrown bricks. The pockmarks caused by these bricks will even fade from the gymnasium floor within a few days.

Townies need to apply to the Gene to serve as brickers. They can leave their applications with the Lu brothers in the jail's lobby. Jail authorities expect a large turnout, Thelma tells me. Gommer groups urge all their members across Town to take part. The loathsome slogan they came up with is this: "Give as good as you got."

I am trying to relate these events to you coolly, Mother and Father. I am trying to stay calm. Yet I am sickened; I am revolted. My heart twinges nonstop, but my tears have all but dried up. I want to speak to Johnny. He must recant what he said at the trial—and so must I. Yet Johnny is refusing to see me, even though he has been granted permission.

I can no longer sleep. At night, I lie in Johnny's bed and have crazy, illogical thoughts. For instance, in my insomniac stupor, I wonder whether Zig might reincarnate Johnny as a new son for you to raise, Mother and Father. It brings me peace of mind to think of you caring for a reincarnated Johnny. He could have my room, my models of Saturn and its moons, my periodic table, my dictionaries of etymology.

On the day before the bricking, there is a knock on my door at seven thirty in the morning. Probably Thelma with some news. But when I open the door, I find Reginald Washington in the hallway.

"Good morning, Boo," Reginald says with a tight smile. "May I call you Boo?"

Even though he said, "may I," I shake my head.

"Oh, sorry, it's just that John calls you Boo all the time."

"You can call me Mr. Dalrymple, Mr. Washington."

I feel oddly jealous that he is in touch with Johnny even though they certainly do not have the blendship that Johnny and I have.

"May I come in for a minute? I have a message from John."

I do not want this weasel here in our private space, but if

he has word from Johnny, I must consent. I wave the council president in and sit on Johnny's unmade bed while Reginald sits on mine.

"I could have sent Tim and Tom Lu, but I thought it best that I deliver this message myself," he says.

I look down. There is a stain of orange pekoe tea on the sleeve of my robe. I am becoming unkempt.

"Mr. Dalrymple, I know you wish to speak to John. Well, he has agreed to see you."

I clap my hands. "Thank Zig," I say.

"There's one condition of John's, however. He wants to speak to you, but, well . . . not right away."

"What do you mean? The bricking is tomorrow night!"

"He wants to speak to you on the basketball court before the . . . beforehand."

The council president cannot muster the courage to say the word "execution."

"He wants to say good-bye, Boo."

I glare at him. The pink starfish-like blotch on his forehead seems larger than before, but this cannot be.

"Mr. Dalrymple"—he corrects himself—"he wants you to be the last person he speaks to."

I cover my face with my hands.

"The situation has been hard on us all," he says. "But let's not forget we're respecting John's wishes. We should take heart in that."

I uncover my face. "You think your intelligence quotient is high and enviable, don't you, Mr. Washington? You are proud of your brains."

He throws me a puzzled look.

"Let me tell you something," I add. "If I had a brick, I'd gladly beat those dear brains of yours out."

He stares, looking scared, as though I might pull a rock-

filled flashlight from under Johnny's pillow. There is no flashlight, but there is a little revolver hidden under the mattress of
Johnny's bed.

"I accept your anger," he says, one hand up to his heart. "I
understand your pain."

"Vamoose!" I say, a word I adore but have little occasion to
use. (Etymology: a bastardized pronunciation of the Spanish
vamos, which means "let us go.")

Reginald pats his knees. He stands. "Please do come," he
says. Then he lets himself out and closes the door behind him.

I remain sitting on Johnny's bed. Unlike the princess with
the pea under her mattress, I cannot feel the lump. I get up and
lift the corner of the mattress. "Hello, my little pretty," I say. I
take the revolver out of its hiding place and cup it in my hands.
It nestles there like a giant death's head cockroach.

The revolver is loaded. The bullets, of course, fit perfectly.

Nd

Neodymium

"THROW RICE, NOT BRICKS" IS THE SLOGAN OF A PACIFIST GROUP that sprang up to oppose Johnny's redeath penalty. Group members encourage couples across Town to tie the knot, to off-set hatred with love. I have never discussed love before because it is not a topic as fascinating as, say, electricity and garbage chutes. But, yes, two townies can fall in love and even wed here. They hold their wedding at a house of good with a member of the do-good council as their priest. Pledges of "I do" are exchanged, confetti is thrown, and tin cans are tied to the backs of bicycles.

Esther considers the wedding campaign lame. Nonetheless, she sits beside me with a plastic Baggie filled with rice dyed pink. I have a Baggie of blue rice. We are in the chapel of the Jonathan Livingston House of Good, where Liz McDougall, the vice president of the do-good council from Eleven, stands on a little stage in a shiny robe that looks to be made out of a theater curtain. "We are gathered here today," she says, "to celebrate the love between Thelma Rudd and Peter Peterman."

When their names are spoken, the bride and groom swing open the doors at the back of the chapel. They march down the center aisle wearing matching macramé vests, which Esther calls hideous—but the party pooper has tears in her eyes. As do I.

When the bride and groom reach the foot of the little stage, Liz McDougall says, "Thelma Rudd, do you take Peter Peterman as your husband and equal and promise to help him remain an honest and upstanding townie in the eyes of Zig?"

Thelma nods her beaded head. "Do I ever!" she exclaims.

"Peter Peterman, do you take Thelma Rudd as your wife and equal and promise to help her remain an honest and upstanding townie in the eyes of Zig?"

"I certainly do."

I always wished I had attended your wedding, Father and Mother, so this day is special to me.

"I now pronounce you husband and wife," Liz McDougall says. "You may kiss!"

Thelma and Peter Peter turn to face the two dozen guests and then peck each other on the lips. People cheer and clap. Esther and I stand and throw fistfuls of rice into the air. It rains down hard on our heads.

The newlyweds lead us all out of the chapel and into the garden at the back of the house of good. Set up under an awning is a table with a bowl of punch and plates of sandwiches. Liz McDougall also serves as the hostess. While Esther is off fetching us food, I sit on the grass beside a bed of daisies and try to think of what to say to Johnny when I see him tonight.

Czar wanders over and sits beside me. He is wearing a T-shirt printed with a tuxedo jacket. His hair is shorter, so now his ears seem to stick out even more. Despite how big they are, they are also thin and delicate. They look as though they might break if I tweaked them.

"Have you found me a portal yet?" he asks.

"Death might be the ultimate portal, Czar."

"Yeah, but once you walk through that door, there's no turning back."

"Some of us don't want to come back."

"You're doing okay here."

"I'm not talking about me. I'm talking about Johnny."

"Listen," he says, "Petey says we're too old to bear grudges.

As usual, he's right. So I want you to know I won't throw bricks tonight. For cripes' sake, I live in a glass house."

How odd that the hypnotist and I have forgiven Johnny, but the gommers have not. I hear they are the only ones who applied to be brickers. They want payback no matter what the cost.

In the middle of the garden is a little gazebo with a shingled roof. Thelma climbs its steps and asks for our attention. "Me and Peter Peter are going to have a bigger party one day to celebrate our wedding. But today's event ain't about us. It's about a boy I met months back. I have a song I want to sing for that boy, Johnny Henzel. May he rest in peace."

Thelma starts singing a song about a new kid in town called Johnny-come-lately, whom everybody loves. While she sings, Czar fishes his blue bauble necklace out from under his tuxedo T-shirt. He takes the necklace off and slips it over my head. The bauble, which is the size of a Susan B. Anthony coin, rests against my heart.

"Wear it tonight, kid," he says. "It'll bring you luck."

61 [144.91]
Pm
Promethium

TONIGHT ZIG CONJURES UP HOLY MACKEREL CLOUDS SO THICK they hide the honey moon that should rightly be Thelma's and Peter Peter's on the eve of their marriage. Yet perhaps a dark, menacing sky is more fitting under the circumstances. After all, no one in our little group (the newlyweds, Esther, and me) is in the mood to celebrate as we bike to the Marcy, guided only by the light of the streetlamps.

Despite the darkness, Thelma insists I wear a hooded sweatshirt with the hood up so that I am less recognizable. She does not want townies badgering me tonight with nosy questions or tactless comments. I also wear overalls, which I chose because they have big pockets to conceal a little revolver.

As the four of us near the Marcy, my holey heart twinges, my intestines knot, and my stomach somersaults. In spite of the late hour, dozens of townies are zooming down the road in the direction of the gymnasium. Those opposed to the redeath penalty are holding a redie-in during which participants will writhe on the ground and scream in feigned agony to protest the bricking. Meanwhile, those foes of Johnny's who cannot stomach the idea of actually wielding bricks will demonstrate outside the Marcy with their usual slogans and placards. As we approach, I spot a gommer carrying a placard that reads, THIS TOWN AIN'T BIG ENOUGH FOR THE BOTH OF US.

The two groups are gathering at opposite ends of the Marcy's lit softball field. It would be thoughtful of me to go thank the hundreds of opponents of the bricking, but Thelma disagrees. She fears my presence on the field might trigger a scuffle between the opposing camps, so we ride past both groups and park our bicycles in the Marcy's circular driveway next to a hedge of evergreens—each bush trimmed, regrettably, in the shape of a bullet.

Johnny Henzel is already inside. This morning, he was transferred here, tied again to a stretcher. I wonder if his jailers are detaining him in the janitor's office in the bowels of the building. If so, has he thought fondly of the time he spent in that room with me?

The three hundred brickers are also already inside the Marcy. At the door to the sports center stands a line of jailers, burly pubescent boys in purple armbands who will allow inside only those townies whose names appear on official lists. Those lists are in the possession of Tim and Tom Lu. The twins have donned T-shirts decorated with the zodiac symbol for Gemini.

Tom says, "Overalls and a hooded sweatshirt. That's not a very attractive look, is it, Tim?"

I lower my hood.

"It's the murder victim, Tom. And now he's also a fashion victim."

"Poor, poor boy," Tom replies. "He'll never recover from the strain he's been under."

"Mark my words," Tim says. "He'll end up at the Deborah."

"Shut your traps!" Thelma cries, a hand raised in the air. "Or I'll smack your faces so hard you'll be looking backward."

"My, that sounds like a threat," says Tom.

"Oh, what a violent world we live in," says Tim.

"In the end, we are all truly victims," says Tom.

Thelma narrows her eyes at the boys, and they finally pipe down. Since the names of my traveling companions are not on the official lists, Esther, Thelma, and Peter Peter must now bid me good-bye and go join the bricking opponents on the softball field, where they, too, will squirm on the ground in mock death throes as part of the redie-in.

Thelma cups my cheeks in her palms the way you used to, Mother. She says, "Mama has faith in you, child."

Old boy Peter Peter says, "Whatever you do, son, you'll do us proud." He ruffles my hair the way you used to, Father.

Esther pulls me aside and gives me an almost embarrassed look. Her cheeks are flushed. Finally, she says, "Give Johnny my love, okay?" Then, because I am still averse to hugs, she gives me a light kick in the shins, what she calls a "love tap." I return the kick. Then Peter Peter and Thelma join in, and under the puzzled gaze of the evil twins and the jailers, my friends and I stand at the entrance to the gymnasium kicking one another.

When I finally pull myself away from my makeshift family and walk into the Marcy, I have the curious feeling—call it a sixth sense—that I am off to meet my maker.

THE BRICKERS WEAR PILLOWCASES OVER THEIR HEADS WITH eyeholes cut out. Their droopy hoods make them look like a slovenly offshoot of the Ku Klux Klan. They stand immobile, hand in hand, on the overhead track, all three hundred of them. They wear gym shorts, T-shirts, and ringed knee socks as if a bricking in a gymnasium were a real sporting event. Under their hoods, are they sweating? Are they queasy and woozy? Are they already regretting the part they will play tonight? Or are they so bloodthirsty they can hardly wait for my part to end and for theirs to begin?

I stand alone in the center circle of the basketball court where Reginald leaves me. The lights overhead are bright and cheery, as though the Trojan basketball team from Helen Keller will soon burst from the locker room and Cynthia Orwell and her cheerleading squad will shake their pompoms and do the splits. Shall I attempt cartwheels and backflips to entertain the brickers as they wait? From where I stand, I cannot see the bricks stacked on the overhead track, but I know they are there somewhere. Six hundred bricks. Two bricks apiece. Enough bricks to bash in the brain of the only Trojan who will emerge from the locker room.

Casper the Friendly Ghost reads eleven forty. In a few minutes, Johnny Henzel will be led out. He and I will have fifteen minutes together before the clock strikes midnight and the bricks fly.

Why has Zig himself not put a stop to this folly? Has he no shame? No wisdom? No superpowers? What is the use of a god without superpowers? Zig's only response so far has been to put the ball in my court. Or the bullets, I should say. Two bullets are inside the little revolver that lies in the left pocket of my overalls. I feared that the jailers might search me, but they did not. Ringo, in fact, even wished me luck earlier. While Reginald was preoccupied, the British jailer leaned in close and gave me a fixed look. "I will miss Johnny boy," he whispered. "I sometimes played my guitar outside his cell door so he'd feel less lonesome. I'd even take his special requests."

Now, as I wait, I stick my hand in my pocket and stroke the little revolver with the tip of a finger, just as Johnny would stroke his roach's back. Around my neck I wear Czar's blue bauble. It lies against my heart under my sweatshirt.

Up on the running track, one of the brickers breaks from the ranks and hurries down the track toward the exit sign. A moment later, three more brickers do likewise. The brickers on either side of the gaps move together and clasp each other's hands again to close the circle. Reginald told me some brickers might drop out at the last minute. Consequently, jail authorities signed up alternates to step in as needed. Soon the four hooded alternates appear along the track and squeeze into the ring.

Casper the Friendly Ghost reads eleven forty-five.

"Red Rover, Red Rover," I mutter, stroking the revolver, "send Johnny right over."

As you know, Mother and Father, I do not usually perspire, but I am sweating now, so much so I must smell as oniony as my old roommate.

The doors to the boys' locker room open, and Johnny and Reginald appear. Johnny is barefoot and bare-chested. He wears only gym shorts, plus cuffs around his ankles and wrists. Reginald, in gym clothes, wears a pillowcase over his head and a whistle around his neck. He grasps Johnny by the arm and leads him toward me in a slow shuffle. The expression "dead man's walk" comes to mind.

When the two boys reach the center circle, Johnny nods at me. Reginald helps Johnny kneel, a clumsy movement given the two pairs of cuffs. Johnny almost keels over, but Reginald pulls him up. I kneel, too, just in front of Johnny. Reginald blinks at me through his eyeholes and then he gives Johnny a pat on the head as a master would do to his basset hound. Without a word, the do-good president retreats back to the doorway of the locker room, where he will stand watch.

I stare at Johnny, who glances up at the three hundred brickers on the overhead track above us. They are not allowed to talk, but a few emit coughs. One hacks so violently I should lend him my new CO_2 bag, which is in the right pocket of my overalls.

Johnny's cheeks are pimply, and his lips are chapped. He leans toward me and, in a near whisper, says, "At my trial, I said one thing that was really true."

"What?"

"You're strong and smart and pure. Don't forget that, even when I'm not around anymore to remind you. Promise me."

My heart twinges. "Promise."

"A lot of what I said was bullsh*t. Talking to Zig, killing Willa, all bullsh*t. But you knew that already 'cause you're smart."

"I know Gunboy is not you. Not the real you."

He smirks and says, "There's a little Gunboy in all of us."

"Johnny, I have a gun with me *now*. The one from Curios." I pat the lump in my left pocket. "I found bullets. Two bullets."

His eyebrows raise. "Really?"

I nod.

"Well, that's perfect." Looking up, he calls out, "Thank Zig!"

I am startled by *Blaberus craniifer*, which suddenly climbs out of the pocket of Johnny's shorts, scurries up his chest and neck, and then burrows into his tangled hair. I glance up at the brickers and over at Reginald, but nobody seems to have noticed.

Johnny seems unfazed that a roach is crawling across his scalp. "Zig never talks to me," he says. "I wish he would, but the b*stard has never said two words to me. Though I think those bullets of yours count as two words."

I am afraid he may be right.

"But Zig gave me Rover, and the roach talks. Remember I thought the voice was Willa's? Well, in jail the whispering got louder and clearer, and I realized who it is."

"Who?"

He leans closer and bores his eyes into mine. "The people in my hospital room. My sister mostly. My folks too. Sometimes a nurse or doctor. I can hear *them*, but they can't hear me."

He has been hallucinating, just like Thelma when she stopped eating and saw toucans in the trees. "Oh, Johnny, you are not in a hospital anymore," I insist. "Your mind is playing tricks."

"I'm alive down in America!" he says, eyes flashing. "I died, you see. But only for a few minutes. My heart stopped beating, but the doctors got it pumping again. I came back to life and I'm getting stronger, but I'm still comatose. I just gotta wake up now. And to wake up there, I can't be alive here, you understand?"

The cockroach emerges from his hairline and perches above his left eyebrow.

"I can hear Brenda right now," he says, glancing up to Rover. "She's saying, 'Come on, Johnny. Open your eyes!'"

I do not know what to say. My heart shudders. My breathing

goes shallow. My eyes water. The tears drip, and I wipe them away with my thumbs.

"Oh, don't be sad for me, Boo," he says in a kind voice. "I'm going home. I'm going back to our old hometown. Everything will be hunky-dory."

He is as mad as Willa with her suicide leap to America. And, what is worse, I want to share in this madness. "Can I go with you?" I say, my voice breaking.

"No, man, you gotta stay in Town."

"Do not leave me alone!" I beg.

"You aren't alone. You got Thelma and Esther and you'll make new friends."

"I do not make friends easily. I am an oddball."

"You gotta stay, 'cause you're dead. Sorry, man, but you're really truly doorknob dead."

He squirms, trying to get comfortable despite the cuffs restraining his wrists and ankles. When he settles down, he says, "I'll get another chance at life, Boo. A real life."

Rover beetles across his forehead and burrows back into his hair. It is eerie how calm Johnny looks, whereas my hair must be standing straight up and my skin must be albino white. "I am really scared," I say. "Aren't you?"

"I don't think it'll hurt much," he says. "I was expecting hundreds of bricks. A bullet will sure as hell hurt a lot less."

A deep sigh from me. "I can't. I . . ."

"Well, *I* can't. Not in cuffs. So you got to."

I start crying again. I glance over at Reginald Washington in the doorway to the locker room, but given the pillowcase, I cannot gauge his reaction.

"There are two bullets left," I say pleadingly. "Two. One for you, one for me."

"Don't be an idiot!" he cries. Lowering his voice, he says,

"You're dead, man. There's no bullet for you! You must've got two in case the first don't work. Understand? Shoot me in the heart, and if I don't disappear right away, shoot me in the head."

I take out the CO_2 bag and hold it to my mouth. I inhale and exhale, and the bag puffs up and crinkles back down with my breath.

"Listen," he says, his voice gentler now. "We never got a chance to know each other too good down in America. But up in Town, we got to be best friends. Aren't we best friends?"

I nod as I breathe into my bag.

"Well, only my best friend can do this for me."

I stop breathing into the bag. "Please don't make me."

My voice is shrill, childish. I am too weak. I am far too weak.

Johnny closes his eyes. When he opens them again, a tear trickles down his cheek. I reach up and wipe it with my thumb. He flinches at my touch.

"Give me a hug. You can do it. And while we're hugging, you take out the gun and you slip it between us so nobody else sees. You point it at my heart." He glances down at his chest, the bull's-eye. "Then you just pull the trigger, and get out of here. Easy as peach pie."

My tears give way to racking sobs. Snot drips from my nostrils and runs into my mouth. I wipe my lips. I wipe my face. I jab my fingertips into the corners of my eyes.

"Help me go home," Johnny says softly. "Help me grow up. Help me get past thirteen."

I pinch the skin on my arm to control my sobs. There are footsteps overhead: more brickers are quitting their jobs. Perhaps if I sob loudly enough, I will drive them all away. But I will never drive them all away. If I do not shoot Johnny, he will die in any case, but in a much ghastlier manner.

Johnny smiles at me, and a dimple pocks his cheek. His eyes are not smiling, though. The whites of his eyes are red.

"Please," Johnny whispers.

And so I lean toward my mad blood brother. I hug him to me. His body smells as oniony as my own. His skin feels feverish, and yet *I* shiver.

The death's head has scrambled down his neck and now perches on his shoulder, like a fairy in a children's book.

I slip my hand into the pocket of my overalls.

"Thank you, Oliver," Johnny whispers.

I pull out the revolver. "Close your eyes, dear Johnny," I say into his ear.

His eyelids clamp shut. His face grimaces. His whole body tenses. I pull back a little. I point the gun at his skinny chest. My hand does not even shake.

"Zig have mercy," I mutter.

I pull the trigger.

63 **151.96**

Eu

Europium

JOHNNY HENZEL DOES NOT VANISH. INSTEAD, HIS BODY FALLS backward in the center circle. His head smacks against the floor. The brickers, seemingly all three hundred of them, gasp together in the echo of the bang. Some yell, *"No! No!"* as I lift the revolver to shoot again, this time pointing at Johnny's head. A bricker flings a brick and hits me in the thigh just as the gun goes off. The bullet misses Johnny and ricochets off the floor. Reginald is running toward me. He stumbles, falls, and rolls, the pillowcase slipping off his head. "I've been shot!" he yells, even though he has not been. Another brick hits the court, breaks in two, and tumbles toward Reginald. He sits up and grabs the whistle from around his neck. His cheeks puff cartoonishly as he blows. The shrillness needles through my brain.

On the overhead track, there is movement and noise and cursing, but I do not glance up. I stare at Johnny. At the red bull's-eye in the center of his chest.

I want to unlock the cuffs from around his ankles and wrists. It must hurt him to lie in such an awkward position. "Do you have the keys to the cuffs?" I call to Reginald, who grasps his ankle, which he twisted in his fall.

"What did you do!?" Reginald whines, his face distorted.

"I killed Johnny," I reply.

"You didn't, you idiot! He's still alive! He's still here!"

I put down the revolver, crawl to Johnny, and lean over him. His eyes are closed. His face is relaxed. There is no tension left. He is as peaceful as an angel. The wound in his chest is the size of a nickel, and the blood looks oddly fake, like the zombie ketchup we townies squirt on ourselves on Halloween.

I place my ear to his chest as dozens of brickers descend into the gymnasium, pulling their pillowcases from their heads. They surround Johnny and me, a few with bricks in their hands as though they may still beat Johnny's brains out, or maybe even mine. Benny Baggarly is here. He picks up the revolver and points it at the ceiling. He pulls the trigger again and again, but of course the gun does not shoot.

The brickers jabber. Reginald groans. Johnny stays silent.

"Please quiet down," I say to the brickers. A few kneel beside Johnny and me as I listen to Johnny's chest.

I sit back up. "There is no heartbeat," I say. "He is redead."

"He's not redead!" Reginald cries out, exasperated. He drags himself toward me through the crowd of brickers. He thinks me mad. I see it in his mean, angry, splotchy face.

At that moment, the death's head scurries out from underneath Johnny and climbs atop his shoulder. A few brickers gasp. Rover sits for a second or two, the death mask on its pronotum seeming to pulsate. And then—*poof!*—the roach disappears into thin air.

I AM SENT TO THE DEBORAH TO RECOVER. A SIX-MONTH STAY imposed on me for my own good by Reginald Washington and his do-good council. Yes, Mother and Father, I have become a sadcon—a third-floor sadcon to be precise, the category of unstable patients forbidden from leaving the asylum grounds. Because I stay calm and collected in the days after I kill Johnny, people assume I am in shock. They tiptoe around me, literally (the ballerina-looking nurse who earlier brought me my breakfast of gruel and English muffin with jam walked as if she were afraid to make the floorboards squeak).

Albert Schmidt, the baby-faced asylum manager, often drops by my room (thankfully, not Willa Blake's old one) to check on me.

"How are you getting on?" he always asks.

"Hunkily-dorily," I reply, coining an adverb.

He does not believe me, of course. Nobody does. I do not even know if I believe myself. I lie on my bed and gaze at the creeping ceiling cracks and twirling ceiling fan, just as I used to do in my room in our apartment, and I miss you both dearly, Mother and Father, and I miss the models of the planets that hung from my ceiling, and I even miss the cobwebs that gathered there because, on my insistence, you gave the spiders the freedom to spin their webs.

Most of all, I miss Johnny.

At least once a day, I go down to the courtyard. I like the courtyard. The sad and confused seem less so here. Bushes blossom with red, yellow, and orange roses. A pergola has trellises overrun with thick vines like those you described in *Jack and the Beanstalk*, Mother. How I regret not having listened raptly when you read me fairy tales in my childhood. Remember how I used to scoff at *The Little Engine That Could* and ask for encyclopedia entries on train combustion? For my limited interest in fictional worlds, I am sorry.

Today when I enter the courtyard, some sadcons are sitting on benches and reading about fictional worlds in novels (*Flowers in the Attic* and *We Have Always Lived in the Castle*). Others are playing gentle games like four square, hopscotch, and jacks. As I stroll by, a few sadcons nod at me or tip their balloon hats. I have become rather famous here. Yet they are too shy to approach and so keep at a safe distance. They think me dodgy and erratic because, despite appearing docile, I did kill a boy.

I sit on my favorite bench. It is my favorite for two reasons. First, it has wise graffiti carved into it: ETERNAL HAPPINESS IS JUST PLAIN CRAZY. Second, it is beside a yellow rosebush whose thorns are sharp. I like to prick a finger and time, with Casper the Friendly Ghost's help, how fast the tiny wound heals. Today my nick takes a mere twenty-two minutes to vanish (a record).

After the nick heals, I look up from my hand and see Esther Haglund coming into the courtyard for a visit. Luckily, she is a full-fledged do-gooder now (third-floor sadcons are allowed visits from do-gooders only). Esther comes weekly to update me on the world outside the Deborah. Today all the sadcons eye her because to match her purple armband, she has on a purple velvet gown—her most flamboyant outfit to date. Zig only knows how she managed to bicycle here. I should ask her to make me a purple velvet suit: if I am to be an oddball, I should look the part.

Esther sits down on my bench, and her feet do not touch the ground. On her feet are slippers with gold sparkles glued to them. She picks a yellow rose and tucks it into her fluffy hair. An artist might capture the beauty of this scene in paint.

"Johnny's still redead, I presume," I say.

Esther nods. Two weeks ago, she told me his body had been taken on a stretcher from the Marcy Lewis Gymnasium to the Sal Paradise Infirmary in Five.

"The nurses still think he'll heal and wake up."

"But his heart isn't beating," I point out.

"They think it'll start up again."

"It never will."

"You don't know that!" she snaps. She rubs her eyes. She looks dumbfounded and frustrated. "Well, if he's redead for good," she asks, "why's this happening? Why's Johnny sticking around?" Her bulbous brow knits. She wants me to solve the puzzle of the first redead townie who does not vanish in the blink of an eye.

"It is a true mystery," I say. "One of my theories is that perhaps Zig believes I need Johnny around, so he left him, or at least part of him, here in Town."

Esther taps my knee, and I wince because I have relapsed into my hands-off policy. "You don't need Johnny anymore, Boo," she says. "We all have to get on with our afterlives without him."

"Oh dear, I can't imagine that," I say.

She stares at me a moment and then shakes her head. "You should start imagining it. Maybe then Zig will let Johnny go."

"No," I simply say, with a shake of my head.

It starts to rain, a light sprinkling at first that nonetheless chases the sadcons and the nurses out of the courtyard and back into the Deborah. Esther stays put even when the rain comes down in cats and dogs and soaks her puffy hair, velvet dress, and sparkly shoes.

We sit and watch the fat raindrops pound the roses. They lose several petals. Yet they are hardy boys (like Frank and Joe, ha-ha), so they will bounce back, I am sure. And so will we, I suppose. I want to share this thought with Esther, but when I turn to her, she looks so wilted that I have my doubts.

She slips off the bench. She pushes her wet hair out of her eyes and gives me a weary look.

"What is it, Esther Haglund?"

"I don't think I'll come back to see you," she says.

I wait in the rain for her to go on, but she just stands there eyeing me as if she has guessed something vital about me that I have not yet figured out myself.

"I know it is not as easy as peach pie to be my friend," I finally say.

She does not reply. She just sighs. Then she turns on her sparkly heels and walks in her bowlegged gait out of my afterlife.

DURING MY TIME AT THE DEBORAH, I TAKE A STILL-LIFE DRAWING
class and, through much practice, learn to sketch vases, bicycles,
desk lamps, pinwheels, typewriters, throw pillows, and the like.
I hone my artistic skills to become a more balanced individual.
I will never be a gifted artist like Johnny, but I am now at least
above average. Next I will graduate to portraits. The first person
I will draw will be Johnny, once I complete my six-month stay.

Sadcons have the option of speaking to a counselor here,
but I opt not to. I do not interact much with the other sadcons
either. In any case, they are wary of me. They conclude that I
am an unlucky friend to have, the same decision Esther has
come to. When I feel lonely, I ask Albert Schmidt to play a
game of chess. Dr. Schmidt, as he is called here, is good at his
job as asylum manager because he does not push anyone to get
better. His policy is to live and let live. He likes having all us
sadcons around. He calls us his children. He is usually kind, but
occasionally grows testy if he does not win at chess, so sometimes I lose on purpose.

I gain roof privileges from Dr. Schmidt after letting him win
several games in a row. At first, I was denied them lest I throw
myself off à la Willa Blake. Once on the roof, I sketch stars in
my notepad and undertake the grueling task of mapping the
night sky. My favorite constellation to date is shaped like an
ankylosaur.

To keep busy, I also volunteer in the kitchen. I like doing
dishes: it is calming to scrape away the remains of our meals

and then soap up our chipped dishes and get them gleaming again. For some reason, Zig has not sent us a dishwasher yet. Perhaps we are not ready for that test.

I also enjoy peeling potatoes. I have even become adept at making sweet potato pie, like the one mentioned in Mother's favorite song, Sarah Vaughan's "It's Crazy." My secret ingredient is the Indian spice garam masala, which I found at the back of the Deborah's pantry. I wish I could make my pie for the both of you. It is much healthier than the pizza pies you scarf down.

To keep fit, I do calisthenics in the courtyard with a Bicentennial sweatband wrapped around my forehead. Dr. Schmidt recommends exercise to combat sadness and confusion. When he spots us exercising, he pretends to be a drill sergeant and cries, "Hup, two, three, four! Hup, two, three, four!" Thankfully, he never attempts to touch us. No pats on the shoulder. No hugs. I think he, too, dislikes being touched. A nurse named Francine, who used to be hard of hearing in America and now still talks too loudly, once laid a hand on his back and he cringed.

Dr. Schmidt died in a school-bus accident. He and three other townies killed in the accident keep in touch and sometimes get together to play Mille Bornes in the games room. He is the grandson of a silent-screen star whose name eludes me since I do not even know the names of current movie stars. I believe, though, that the actress once played Jane in a Tarzan movie.

Even though I respect Dr. Schmidt, he will never become a best friend, not like the blendship I had with Johnny. After all, blendships are rare, as I am sure you two will agree, being in a blendship yourselves.

Johnny is still here in Town, resting in peace at the Sal Paradise Infirmary. His heart is still quiet. The do-good council is unsure what to do with Johnny's body.

Townies sometimes slip into the infirmary to steal peeks at the famous "half-deader," as they call him. Despite the nurses' watch, some townies manage to touch his skin to feel how dry and cool it is. They run a fingertip around the circumference of his chest wound, which has dried but not healed.

I know all this because Czar told me so in a letter. He said he snuck into the Sal himself, and when he saw Johnny's lifeless body and touched his chest wound, he decided to place a blue bauble necklace around my friend's neck. "The poor bugger deserves some magic," he wrote. "Maybe the topaz will kick-start his heart." A noble position, I feel.

Other than Czar and Esther, I have had little contact with the outside world. I refuse other visitors, and now I say no even to Thelma and Peter Peter because I believe they, too, need a break from me. I write them to apologize. They write back, but I do not open that letter, or the later ones they send.

Many strangers also write me. I presume they are gommers. Dr. Schmidt tells me some gommers see me as a hero, while others see me as a nuisance for spoiling their bricking fun. I throw all these letters down the garbage chute unopened.

Esther Haglund does not write and, as she promised, does not visit. I do not write her either. I respect her decision. I miss her, though.

A month before my six-month stay ends, I move to the second floor of the Deborah. Several of my fellow patients and I apply for day passes to work as sorters at a nearby supply warehouse. Zig made an overnight delivery, and I have high hopes of stumbling on another clue from him or instructions—something like the bullets he sent me. I want to know how I should proceed from here because, honestly, I feel adrift. I need some direction to decide what I will do with the rest of my afterlife.

At the warehouse, I drag mattresses and box springs around, load lamps into grocery carts, stack desks on dollies, sort dozens of T-shirts according to size, and fill boxes with art supplies. While I work, I daydream that the warehouse is a portal that will teleport me back to Hoffman Estates, where I can visit you, Mother and Father. Silly, I know.

Some of the sorters pilfer belongings—I see a surly sadcon named Clementine stick a donkey marionette into her knapsack—but I do not steal a thing. In any case, nothing out of the ordinary comes my way that day or the other days I volunteer. Nothing curious. Perhaps I have lost my ability to discern.

Or perhaps Zig is telling me to find my own way, fly on my own angel wings, as it were (ha-ha).

One evening, while I sit on my bed at the Deborah and draw a still life of a scruffy one-eared teddy bear that once shared its life with Willa Blake, an idea pops into my head. I mull it over and decide it is indeed splendid. I know what I ought to do with my afterlife, and with the still life that is Johnny Henzel.

I immediately write Peter Peter in care of Curios. I apologize for my long silence. I ask for my old job back provided he can forgive me for stealing one of his curious objects (the revolver). I arrange to see him and Thelma on the Friday before the Monday of my release from the Deborah.

We meet in the art room, a neutral ground that Dr. Schmidt favors for get-togethers between sadcons and non-sadcons. On the walls of the room, I hang many of my still-life drawings because there is a link between them and the favor I will ask Peter Peter and Thelma.

They show up wearing matching straw hats tied with red ribbons, like those worn by gondoliers. Thelma goes teary-eyed and says, "My baby's lost weight." I tell her she knows as well as I that weight loss is impossible in Town unless a townie lops off, say, his own hand or foot. I tell her she has lost not a single pound since last I saw her, and she hugs her fat stomach tightly, which means she is hugging me.

Peter Peter has a gift for me in an oblong box that looks like the type that fountain pens come in. Inside is not a pen, however. Instead, the gift is a one-of-a-kind newly arrived curious object, a mercury thermometer that shows that the Deborah's art room is seventy-seven degrees Fahrenheit and twenty-five degrees Celsius. Mercury, also known as quicksilver, is element No. 80, abbreviated as Hg.

"I want you to keep the thermometer till you return to work at Curios," Peter Peter says.

"I am touched," I tell them. "Touched in the sense of emotionally moved, not in the sense of slightly mad."

Thelma shows me her gap-toothed smile. Peter Peter chuckles. These people do care about me. It is hard to imagine why at this point in my afterlife.

I tell them my splendid idea.

THREE MONTHS LATER, A NEW EXHIBITION IS SET TO BEGIN ITS run at Curios. It is simply called *Zoo*, like the name of the pet shop Johnny had planned to open one day.

My posters for the exhibition mention that *Zoo* will pay tribute to the late animals that once called Town their home: the gerbil Lars, the budgie Gloria, the kitten Crappy, the roach Rover, and the sea monkeys, which we never bothered to name.

Over the past week, townies have written their names on our sign-up sheet for a guided visit of *Zoo* to be held on Sunday evening. For the event, places are limited to thirteen and reserved on a first-come, first-served basis.

When Sunday evening arrives, I gather my audience in front of the door leading into the exhibition hall that houses *Zoo*. Above the door is a sign painted with a big red *Z*, a big white *O*, and a big blue *O* (the colors are Thelma's idea; she is patriotic). An ornate old bureau is set in front of the door so nobody can slip into *Zoo* before I am ready. When a boy in an NBC peacock T-shirt tries sliding the bureau away, Czar, who now serves as the security guard at Curios, yells, "Get your dirty paws off that, you motherf*cking, assl*cking ignoramus!"

I feel bad for the peacock boy because he and all my visitors tonight are the kind of avid pupils, bookworms, and loners who would spend their lunch hours studying in the library at Helen Keller. In other words, they are versions of yours truly.

When Casper the Friendly Ghost reads eight o'clock, I emerge from a table in the corner, where I have been quietly polishing Susan B. Anthony coins with a toothbrush dipped in white vinegar. I introduce myself as Oliver Dalrymple, their *Zoo* guide this evening.

"Hey, you're that kid!" says a girl who—oddly enough—has the end of her arm shoved inside a sock puppet of a tabby kitten, possibly a likeness of Crappy. When she talks, she makes the kitten's mouth move. "You're Gunboy, aren't you?" she asks.

Townies have begun to call me Gunboy.

"There's a little Gunboy in all of us," I reply.

I nod toward Czar. He begins dragging the bureau away from the door with help from Peter Peter, who has come out of his office to assist.

My guests eye me warily, now that they know who I am. They seem to fear I may draw a revolver and shoot them down.

I open the doors to the exhibition hall and lead them inside. Around the rectangular room are displays commemorating Town's animal life. The gerbil display, for instance, is Lars's former terrarium with its little exercise wheel and water bottle and even a few of his half-chewed toilet rolls, all of which Peter Peter saved because he is a pack rat (or perhaps a pack gerbil, ha-ha).

Now that I, too, am an artist of sorts, I made a faux gerbil using scraps from a leatherette handbag and the brown bristles of old hairbrushes. Posted on a bristol board beside the gerbil display is the story of Lars, mentioning such details as his Latin name (*Meriones unguiculatus*), the zone he was discovered in (Three), the date of his discovery in a crate of tennis balls (September 25, 1974), his favorite food (parsnips), and his life span in heaven years (two years, one month, four days).

Around the room are similar displays for the other creatures.

I made a tabby out of felt and fabric, and a budgie out of yellow and green feather boas.

As for *Blaberus craniifer*, we have plenty of Johnny's drawings, from thumb sketches in India ink to full-page sketches in colored pencil. I made a life-size figurine of the cockroach out of clay and painted a detailed black blotch on its head to replicate the death mask that gives the insect its name.

I still do not understand why Rover vanished instead of Johnny, but perhaps it had simply reached the end of its natural life in heaven. Or perhaps it died of a broken heart (a cockroach's heart, by the way, has thirteen chambers).

My guests listen politely as I give my talk about *Zoo* and the creatures in it. I try to pique their curiosity by telling amusing anecdotes: for example, that Crappy was so named because she was separated from her mother too young and thus took a long time to learn how to use the litter box containing playground sand as her kitty litter (an example of which is on display).

A gloomy-looking fellow, whom somebody called an old boy, says, "We were *all* separated from our mothers too young."

After I finish my talk, I lead my visitors to the end of the exhibition hall, where, hanging from the ceiling, is a red velvet curtain.

"What's behind it? The Wizard of Oz?" says a smart aleck.

I shake my head and draw the curtain to reveal a door leading into a smaller exhibition hall (formerly a storage room). I open the door and guide my visitors inside. It is dark in this second room, and so nobody sees at first what is on display. With the light from Casper the Friendly Ghost, I find the floor lamp and click it on.

"Behold the star attraction," I say.

At the back of the windowless room, lying on a single bed, is a boy. We all approach his bed.

"It's just a kid sleeping," the smart aleck says. "Big whoop!"

"Rise and shine!" says puppet girl, and snaps her free fingers in his face.

"He won't wake up," I tell her.

We all continue staring at the boy in the bed. Nobody makes a sound.

Finally, a fat girl exclaims, "Jeez, it's the half-deader!"

The other twelve visitors also arrive at the same conclusion: before them lies the body of Johnny Henzel.

Johnny Henzel is my splendid idea.

Let me tell you, Mother and Father, that nobody was initially receptive to my plan. I first had to persuade Peter Peter and Thelma, who found the idea a little ghoulish. As for Reginald Washington, well, he wanted me confined to the Deborah for an extra six months simply for *suggesting* my idea. I explained, however, that tucking Johnny away in an infirmary and forgetting about him would do no one any good. We need to remember him. We need to talk about his life here and in America to better understand his story. As a result, we can be better prepared should Zig one day send us another boy like Johnny Henzel.

My aim, you see, is to honor my friend, but also to avoid another bricking of another sadcon.

In the end, Reginald and the do-good council gave my *Zoo* the green light, at least on a trial basis, thanks partly to support the project obtained from warden Lydia Finkle. When I asked Reginald what he meant by "trial basis," he replied, "We'll shut you down, Mr. Dalrymple, if you go mental again."

For opening night, Johnny is wearing cutoff jeans and a tank top printed with Tony the Tiger of Frosted Flakes fame. The blue bauble sits atop the bullet wound. On his feet, he wears gym socks whose bumblebee stripes (yellow and black) are the Helen Keller colors.

His eyes are closed. He does not look peaceful, nor does he look in pain. He looks absorbed, as if he is figuring out a tricky arithmetic problem in his head.

Czar comes into the hall and warns visitors not to get too close to Johnny. "Don't smother the guy, folks," he orders. "Give him some air."

"We can't smother somebody who isn't alive," say the girl and Crappy 2.

"Hello there, Johnny," I say, leaning over the bed. "How are you doing this fine evening?" I do not expect an answer. If he did blink open his eyes and say, "Hunky-dory," thirteen townies might develop their own holey hearts (ha-ha).

Around the room, I posted all of Johnny's drawings and paintings that I could gather together. He had done portraits and caricatures of Esther, Thelma, and me, as well as his parents and Brenda, his jailer Ringo, his basset hound—and of course Gunboy. He drew dorms (the Frank and Joe), trees, bicycles, warehouses, jungle gyms, basketball nets, dandelions, even a row of urinals.

I give my thirteen visitors the facts that I recall from Johnny's life in Hoffman Estates and from his afterlife in Town. I do not hide embarrassing details. I tell them I now suspect that the camp (the infamous Squeaky Fromme) he attended in the summer before our passing was actually a kind of mental asylum like the Deborah.

Since it is too late for mercy, I try to elicit sympathy for my friend. I tell my audience that a troubled mind can cause a boy to do strange things. "He had an illness as serious as the cancer that felled certain thirteen-year-olds before they came to Town," I say.

I allow the visitors to touch Johnny's arms and legs. "Gross!" the fat girl cries, but the others take turns running a hand along his limbs. They tell me his skin is cool.

"Does he have rigor mortis?" the old boy asks.

"Good question," I say. "But no, he does not." To prove this, I lift one of his arms and bend it back and forth at the elbow.

"Is he in a coma?" asks a boy with a walleye (strabismus).

"No, the comatose still have functioning hearts, whereas Johnny's is as quiet as a piece of lapis lazuli." I refer to lapis lazuli in particular because its name translates as "stone of heaven."

"Is the bullet still in him?" the same boy asks.

I move the fake topaz away from his dented wound. The dried blood is almost black.

"The bullet hasn't resurfaced," I tell my guests.

The hand-puppet girl suggests that Johnny's bullet may have dissolved, and I admit she may be right. "Can we see the gun?" she asks.

There are drawers that slide out from beneath the bed. Two are used to store extra clothes because I change Johnny's tank top, shorts, socks, and boxers weekly, with Czar's help. Even though Johnny no longer sweats, he retains an oniony odor, but it is so faint I have to put my nose almost against his scalp to detect it.

Another drawer contains the revolver. I open it and pull out the gun. Several of the visitors gasp. The fat girl clasps her hands over her mouth.

The smart aleck says, "It ain't loaded, I hope," but he has an excited look that says otherwise.

I pass the revolver around. Some of my guests take it as though it were a hot potato or a grenade set to go off.

The puppet girl holds Crappy 2 close to my face. One of its button eyes is coming loose, the black thread hanging like an optic nerve. "When you pointed that gun at your friend's chest," Crappy 2 says, "what was going through your mind?"

"It may sound strange for me to say so," I answer, "but I thought I was saving Johnny."

"Maybe when he shot you," Crappy 2 replies, "Johnny thought he was saving you too."

72	178.49
Hf	
Hafnium	

LATER THAT EVENING, AFTER EVERYONE HAS LEFT CURIOS, I AM sweeping the floor in Johnny's room when I hear footsteps in *Zoo*. The red velvet curtain is pushed aside, and there stands Esther Haglund in the doorway. She is wearing a shiny white dress, and her hair is piled atop her head in ringlets.

"Wow, you look just like an angel, Esther," I say. I have not seen her since my early days at the Deborah.

"I want to show Johnny I made an effort," she says, smoothing out the front of her dress. "It's taffeta, but not real silk. Unfortunately, that b*stard Zig is stingy with his silk."

I heard from Thelma that Esther moved to Three, where she now makes clothes for other townies, with help—believe it or not—from former jailer Ringo, who finally quit his job at the Gene to become a tailor.

Thelma must have told Esther about *Zoo* and its main attraction. My old friend goes over and sits on the side of Johnny's bed and, with a deep sigh, touches a finger to the bridge of his nose, just as I once did to dearly departed Uncle Seymour.

I wonder if Esther was in love with Johnny Henzel. Perhaps that is why she needed time away from him and me. I picture the broken plastic heart from the Operation game in her chest, and my eyes tear up, something they have not done in some time. I turn away so Esther does not see me.

"Excuse me a minute, Esther. I need to fetch something from my office," I say, to give her time alone with Johnny.

In my office, I sit at my desk. A blank sheet of paper is in my typewriter. I have been working again on the story of my afterlife. I have finally reached the present day and am not sure where the story goes next.

No one has read my story yet. I wanted you to be the first, Mother and Father. The pages of my manuscript are in a three-ringed binder kept in a locked drawer of my desk. I fetch the drawer key from inside the base of the Wobblin' Goblin music box, open the drawer, and take out the binder. On my way out of my office, I also grab the box of Lucky Charms from a crowded shelf. Peter Peter will be cross if we eat the cereal, but so be it. Given all we have been through, Esther and I deserve this gift from Zig.

She and I sit on threadbare armchairs we drag into Johnny's *Zoo* room. We share the box of cereal, our hands digging in search of the marshmallows in the shapes of hearts, moons, stars, clovers, and diamonds. Esther finds the prize at the bottom of the box: an elf figurine. She gives it to me. "Elves are my f*cking bête noire," she says. "Back in Utah, I was always asked to play one in the Christmas pageant."

As we snack, I read the story of my afterlife aloud. To Esther, but also to Johnny. My blood brother still has a concentrated look on his face as though he is trying to figure out what our story means.

Sometimes during my reading Esther stops me to make a correction or clarify some aspect of our adventures. She nods her head a lot and even says "Amen," the way I imagine Christians do in church when ministers read from their Bible.

I read up to the part where Esther arrives at *Zoo*. It is three fifteen by this time. My voice is going hoarse. Esther's eyes are blinking shut, and her ringlets have come undone. "It's time you put this baby to bed," she says.

I assume she means she is the baby who is ready for bed (we will have to sleep on sofas at Curios tonight), but then she clarifies: "Go finish this chapter and then come read it to me."

So that is what I do.

HERE IS ONE MORE CHAPTER, DEAR MOTHER AND FATHER. IT IS dedicated to you, as is every page herein. I have gradually lost faith that I will ever find a way to deliver to you the story of my afterlife, and so I will stop for now and say good-bye. I want to stop while I still remember what the two of you look like. In time, your faces will grow dimmer and dimmer. It will be as though you died instead of me. But even when I cannot see your faces anymore, please know this: your son still loves you. How curious that I never told you so before.

74	183.84
W	
Tungsten	

75	186.21
Re	
Rhenium	

76	190.23
Os	
Osmium	

77	192.22
Ir	
Iridium	

78	195.08
Pt	
Platinum	

79	196.97
Au	
Gold	

80	200.59
Hg	
Mercury	

81	204.38
Tl	
Thallium	

95 [243.06]

Am

Americium

DEAR FATHER AND MOTHER, I HAVE NOW LIVED IN TOWN AS LONG as I lived in America: thirteen years. I am no longer a newbie. It is hard to believe I ever was. Yet I have changed little in the intervening years. After all, we townies idle. Thelma Rudd claims I am now more mature. Perhaps, but I do not feel so.

Over the years, I have continued to live at the Frank and Joe and to do the same work at Curios. I am now the museum's curator, a position I inherited when dear Peter Peter repassed more than eight years ago.

Thelma held a wake as Peter Peter approached fifty years old. A wake in Town, however, is different from a wake in America. In our wakes, we five-decade-old townies are not yet dead (or redead). Each night as we near fifty, our friends gather in our room. Zig does not necessarily steal us away on the exact date of our fiftieth rebirthday; we may disappear a week or two before or after this date (in the same way that a pregnant lady in America does not necessarily deliver *exactly* nine months after conception). During his wake, Peter Peter's friends sat cramped together around his bed and talked. Peter Peter lay under the covers listening. One night he closed his eyes . . . and *poof.* No fade-out. No fifty-year aging all at once. Thelma screamed (though she had promised Peter Peter she would stay calm).

The other old boy, Peter Peter's friend Czar, refused to have a wake. He said it was embarrassing to have people watch you redic. He said it was akin to having people watch you "take a crap." As a result, he forbade anyone from being present in his room when he repassed, two months after Peter Peter.

Over the years, I have kept myself busy with various projects. I teach a constellation class at the Franny Glass School in Thirteen. After my first five years in Town, Zig changed the night sky backdrop, and thus I needed to start mapping anew. As time passes in heaven, the stars do not change places, not till the day when Zig changes the complete backdrop. I tell my students this is a metaphor for life: we go along thinking nothing will be different, till the day everything suddenly changes at once.

One morning about six years ago, a kite sailed in over the South Wall in Seven. Because the kite is red with one big yellow star and four smaller yellow stars, the design of the Chinese flag, certain townies believed it came from Chinese thirteen-year-olds in a nearby terrarium. Sadly, no note was tied to its tail, so we are unsure of its origin, but at least it gave us proof we are not alone. The "Chinese" kite is now on display in Hall 3 at Curios.

Four years ago, a large upper section of the Southwest Corner in Six crumbled, severely injuring several townies gathered at the bottom of the wall for a folk festival dedicated to the music of Bob Dylan. Was this incident intentional on Zig's part (perhaps not a fan of Mr. Dylan's work) or simple neglect? Some think the former; I presume the latter. The damaged wall grew back within sixteen days, by which time all of the injured had been released from the Paul Atreides Infirmary in Seven.

Some changes have been on a smaller scale. Guess what! We have a dog, a French poodle that arrived only two months ago in a warehouse located just down the street from Curios. Pierre (named by Thelma in honor of Peter Peter) has a woolly chocolate coat, which we do not clip, and a little pink tongue, the tip of which often sticks out of his mouth. His favorite foods are black-eyed peas, carrot greens, and butternut squash, and, thank Zig, this carnivore thrives on a vegetarian diet, though of course he will grow no bigger. He will idle like the rest of us.

I could continue citing other interesting developments in Town in the intervening years, but let us move on to the reason I am writing to you again after such a long pause.

Something magical is happening in Town, and it has renewed my faith that I may eventually manage to deliver my story to you.

The magic involves Johnny Henzel.

For many years, Johnny played a much smaller role in my afterlife. Yes, I continued to check on him and change his clothes as needed, but for a long time he did not occupy my thoughts the way he had during my first year or two here.

There is an old wives' tale in America that hair and fingernails keep growing after a person's death. In the case of townies, ours do, but in the case of Johnny, this was false. In the years he lay in bed at *Zoo*, his hair stayed the same length it was on the day I shot him: four inches at its longest. Yet last week, while changing his clothes, I noticed his hair seemed longer. I fetched my ruler and measured: five and a third inches. Then I spotted his fingernails. Before his redeath, he had chewed them down to the quick, so imagine my shock when I saw crescent moons appearing where no nails had been before.

My old friend is growing.

Johnny Henzel goes from five feet three to five feet four, then five five, then five six. The peach fuzz above his lip and on his chin turns into dark whiskers. Dark hair also sprouts along his arms and legs, in his armpits, and in his pubic region.

For a few days, I shave his face with the electric razor displayed in Hall 2, but then I abandon this ploy. Instead, I close off his room at *Zoo* with a heavy armoire and lie that I am redesigning the space to boost attendance. People believe me because over the years Johnny has drawn fewer and fewer visitors. Most townies have seen him. They know his story; he is old news. Johnny would, however, attract hordes of bedazzled townies if they knew he was the first among us to grow past age thirteen.

"What is this magic?" I ask Johnny as I dab acne cream on a pimple on his cheek. I slip a thermometer into his mouth to see whether there is a change in his normal body temperature of ninety-six degrees. He has never grown cold. He has always felt as though he died only five minutes before, but now his temperature has risen a degree.

I close down Curios altogether, with the excuse that I am planning a major revamp, and do not allow others on the premises at all. I stay here practically around the clock, zipping out only to pick up takeout meals at a cafeteria.

I claim I need my solitude. Only Pierre stays behind to keep me company. When townies ask about my design plans, I remain vague. I speak of flowing creative juices, a visiting muse. The artistic townies eat up such talk, including Thelma, who pats my head encouragingly. Esther, though, looks doubtful. "What are you scheming?" she asks, narrowing her eyes. Yet even she leaves me alone since she is busy planning her wedding. She will marry her tailor partner, Ringo (whose real name, by the way, is Nigel Bell).

Once Curios is closed down, I move sofa cushions into Johnny's room to sleep on. We are roommates again. Given Johnny's steady growth, I change his clothes often. I have to wrestle with his big lanky body. His arms and legs are gangly, his feet long, his toes pointy. I clip his fingernails and toenails daily but no longer trim his hair. His hair and beard grow as long as a flower-power hippie's. His chest fills out, making his bull's-eye wound look smaller.

I watch him age about a year every two days, and soon he is Town's first real man. His body grows to six feet one inch and stops. He keeps aging, though. I see the changes mostly in his face; all the baby fat in his cheeks melts away, and his cheekbones stand out. I estimate he is nearing twenty-six years old, the same age he would be if he were still in America.

I think he may be handsome, but I am not sure: I have always had trouble seeing beauty in human beings. What I find beautiful—a crop of pimples in the pattern of an ankylosaur constellation, for example—others find repugnant.

Every day, I lift his eyelids to check his pupils, but they remain dilated and motionless. I put my ear to his chest. His heart offers not one chug.

One evening, as I am examining him, I see something frightening: a red pool spreading out beneath his left palm. I grab his hand, turn it over. His left wrist has been slashed several times. Blood seeps from the gashes and runs down his arm.

Then I notice his right wrist. It, too, is oozing blood.

I yank open the drawer beneath his bed, pull out an old T-shirt, dab at the blood. Within minutes, the gashes on both wrists have scabbed over.

"What in hell's name is going on?" I say aloud.

96 [247.07]

Cm

Curium

AT FIVE IN THE MORNING ON SEPTEMBER 7 (MY REBIRTHDAY), I slink out to a supply warehouse to filch some clothing for Johnny. It has been about five weeks since he began to grow. I hope to find him some extra-large gym shorts and tank tops, the kind made for the biggest boys among us. As a precaution, I fill my flashlight with rocks. Zig knows what type of enemy I may encounter in these strange and uncertain times. I still do not understand how Johnny's wrists bled. His scabs have healed, but deep zigzag scars linger.

I head off to the warehouse, one hand on my flashlight, the other holding Pierre's leash. The dog scurries down the sidewalk, tugging surprisingly hard for such a small creature.

As I approach the warehouse on Carrie White Street, the two quarter-pie windows above the warehouse doors go from dark to bright. Whenever a delivery comes in, Zig automatically turns on the lights as a kind of beacon to us townies. *Perfect,* I think. *I will have first dibs before the sorters arrive at eight thirty.*

Outside the warehouse are two security guards sitting on overturned buckets and playing crazy eights on a wobbly card table. They are used to my visits. As curator at Curios, I have a special pass to visit warehouses in search of curious objects. The guards barely glance up from their game, despite the presence of Pierre, who usually elicits so much cooing and fussing from passersby that I tend to walk him only early in the morning or late at night.

I grasp the metal door handle, heave the door open, and slip inside the warehouse. I unhook Pierre from his leash so he can scramble over the hoard of goods Zig has bestowed on us. As usual, the delivery looks like a yard sale of unwanted, unloved items: used desks, mattresses, and stoves; piles of secondhand T-shirts; a jumble of compact discs; boxes of paperback books, their corners curled with age; even a half dozen scratched, tarnished tubas, their mouths all facing one another as though they are conversing.

I am on my knees riffling through a box of secondhand gym shorts when I hear Pierre's sharp yaps coming from the other side of the warehouse.

Pierre can do a trick whereby he throws back his head and imitates the *wee-ooo-wee-ooo* sound of a European police siren. We tell ourselves he learned this in the streets of Paris. Everybody loves it when he does his trick. I myself find his howl grating, and so when he starts up in the warehouse now, I put down my armful of gym shorts and go to shut him up.

I spot him in front of an old school locker that stands upright between a refrigerator and a photocopier. He is pawing the locker between howls. Pierre arrived in a cardboard box of throw cushions himself, and perhaps this locker contains another dog or a cat or even Town's first raccoon. As I approach the locker, however, I realize there is something familiar about it: a dent halfway up its army green surface, as though a student's head was once butted against its door.

It is then I notice the number on the metal plate near the top. It is 106. "Holy smokes," I say to Pierre, who finally stops his barking.

"What kind of tomfoolery are you up to, Zig?" I say aloud as I touch a palm against the locker's cool surface. What will I find inside? The periodic table? Photographs of

Richard Dawkins and Jane Goodall? My old gym clothes? My protractor?

As I inch the locker door open, its rusty hinges let out a series of squeaks that, considering my nerves, could also be coming from me.

Inside the locker is a face I have not seen in thirteen years.

THE LOCKER ITSELF IS EMPTY, BUT ITS REAR PANEL IS MISSING, and, instead of revealing the back of the warehouse, the space opens onto a hallway where there hangs a black-and-white portrait of a blind and deaf high-school graduate wearing a mortarboard on her head.

In the years since I last saw Helen Keller, she has not changed one iota. She has been locked in time like me. She gives me an encouraging look, as encouraging a look as a blind lady can. "Come along now, child," she seems to say. "Don't be afraid."

Helen faced many ordeals in her life boldly and bravely, and so must I. I look down at Pierre. He looks up, wet-eyed, tongue tip sticking out. He emits a low squeal.

"Stay," I say to him. "I'll be back."

Will I, though?

I wedge myself into the portal before me. I know I will fit: Jermaine Tucker once shut me inside this very locker. I close the door behind me so that Pierre cannot climb through. Just as I slip out of the locker and into the hallway of my old school, the bell rings. Hordes of students spill from the classrooms up and down the corridor. For a moment, I am frozen. My heartbeat quickens because I fear seeing Jermaine Tucker, Kevin Stein, Henry Axworthy, and their ilk—but of course I do not. I do not recognize any of the seventh graders and eighth graders jabbering and cursing and giggling and roughhousing. Thirteen years have passed.

Am I invisible? I hold my hands to my face. They look pale

but solid. The ghost around my wrist, Casper, now reads three thirty. The bell that rang is the last bell of the day.

"Do you mind?" says an Asian girl with butterfly clips in her hair and a shell necklace around her neck. "You're, like, totally blocking my way."

I am not invisible.

I step aside so the new owner of my old locker can fetch her belongings. Since I stepped out of it, the locker has closed behind me. The girl fiddles with her lock, and I almost ask if the combination is still 7–25–34. But she does not give me a second glance, nor do the other students. Yet the blind Helen seems to. "Get a move on," I imagine her saying. "You have a haunting to do."

I swerve through the crowd as the students jostle one another. Unfurled on a wall is a team banner reading, TROJAN, SLAY THY ENEMY! The walls have been repainted: they were once pale yellow but are now spearmint green.

I pass an empty classroom, the room where I used to study science. On the teacher's desk is a plastic model of the human heart with its chambers, valves, and arteries exposed. I am drawn toward it, but before I can examine the heart, another item attracts my attention. Thumbtacked to a corkboard is, lo and behold, a periodic table. An updated periodic table!

"May I help you?"

I turn around and face a man whose head is bald but whose chest must be furry because a tuft of black hair pokes out of the top of his shirt. I have not seen an adult—other than the grown-up Johnny Henzel—in thirteen years, so I am startled, as though I just stumbled on a bear in the woods.

"Your periodic table," I say to this man whom I do not recognize, "it has one hundred and nine elements now."

The science teacher glances at the periodic table and then looks back at me. "That's right. One hundred and nine, yes."

"I thought there were only one hundred and six. I imagine that"—here I read from the table—"bohrium, hassium, and meitnerium were discovered in the last dozen years."

Speared behind the teacher's ear is a long pencil indented with teeth marks. The man gives me a quizzical look. "Oh, we're making new discoveries all the time," he says. "You never know what'll turn up next."

Peter Peter used to say more or less the same thing about objects destined for Curios.

"Good day to you, sir," I say to the science teacher.

"Good day to you too," the man says, scratching a patch of psoriasis on his elbow.

I turn and walk from the room into the crowded corridor. I am pushed along, past bulletin boards filled with students' reproductions of album art (*Little Earthquakes*, *Lucky Town*, *Nevermind*, *99.9F°*), a poster for auditions for a play (*Death of a Salesman*), and a perplexing campaign flyer for student council (PHIL PRATT IS PHAT!).

Out of the corner of my eye, I glimpse Mr. Miller, my English teacher to whom I taught the difference between "who" and "whom." He now has a potbelly, and his salt-and-pepper hair is now just salt. Another actual adult. I avert my gaze lest he think he has seen a ghost. Down the hall and across the lobby I hurry. As I push through Helen Keller's front doors, I realize that the last time I left this school, I was lying on a stretcher, a blanket thrown over my corpse.

Outside I see so many things I have not seen in a dog's age. Speaking of dogs, at the edge of the school driveway, I see a German shepherd, which runs by me leash-less. I see a dozen sparrows flutter into a tree. Around me are bungalows, automobiles, school buses, mailboxes, stop signs, traffic lights, and convenience stores. How liberating and peculiar to be free of the towering Great Walls that imprison us townies.

My eyes go watery from joy!

As I admire my surroundings, a gray squirrel bounds toward me and stands with its tail twitching and paws limp-wristed. "Thank you, Zig," I say to the squirrel, as though *Sciurus carolinensis* were my god. The animal snatches a maple key and then scrabbles up a tree. I wish it were fall so I could see orange and red maple leaves! I wish it were winter so I could see snow, and perhaps grasp a bumper and skitch down the street!

On the edge of the sidewalk is an anthill teeming with ants. I drop to my knees. I am awed by my little friends' strength and purposefulness. An ant can carry fifty times its body weight. Were I an ant, I could carry an ice-cream truck on my back. I mention such a truck because one passes by, ringing its bell and attracting a Pied Piper line of students. Townies would be envious, since ice cream is not among the foods Zig sends. For a frozen treat, we townies make do with putting peeled bananas in the freezer and then running them through a food processor.

Compared with Town, Hoffman Estates has such a variety of humans! After thirteen years of nothing but thirteen-year-olds, it is heavenly (ha-ha) to see, for example, an old man walking with a cane. How old is he? Sadly, I can no longer tell age. Sixty-two? Eighty-nine? Running beneath the translucent skin on his forearms are whole tributaries of snaky blue veins, so he must be very old.

"It's beautiful out, *n'est-ce pas*?" I say to the man, whose nose has the same texture as cauliflower.

He looks up. An airplane is passing, creating contrails across the wild blue yonder. "The sky used to be bluer in my day," he says.

"But it *is* your day," I reply. "You aren't dead yet."

The next person I pass is a man in a tank top with ballooning muscles like a cartoon superhero's. Then I see a shawled lady pushing an actual toddler in a stroller. In the child's hair is clamped a swarm of bumblebee barrettes. As you know, I was never fond of young children because conversing with them is dull, yet I actually babble "Gitchy gitchy goo!" at the child.

I must stop all this staring at my surroundings and make haste. Who knows how long this haunting will last? I once thought a haunting would be unfair to you, cruel even. I have changed my mind. Perhaps I am being selfish, but I want to see your faces again. Zig willing, I will.

I start running. I am a speed demon. I intend to head straight for Clippers, since at this time of the day that is where you should be, but since Sandpits is on the way, I cut through our apartment complex. I take Hill Drive, and I am huffing and puffing by the time I reach 222. I stop and glance at the second-floor balcony. Through the balcony door, I glimpse movement, a person walking past. You may be home early! Or perhaps you have taken the day off because it is the anniversary of my death.

I hurry up the walkway and into our low-rise. When I reach Apartment 6 on the second floor, I see on our door a wreath made of sticks twisted together with little plastic cardinals nesting within. Mother, you must have made it in one of your arts and crafts workshops. I bang the door knocker without thinking what I will say if you answer and find your late son standing before you. I do not have time to think because I fear that Zig will reel me back any second—perhaps even the very second I glimpse your faces and you glimpse mine. Perhaps when the door swings open, I will vanish and you will have the ghost of your son burned on your retinas as your only proof I was ever there.

But when the door swings open, you are not whom I see. Whom I see is an older teenager with a nest of messy black hair. He wears a black T-shirt with the name ROBERT SMITH written across the chest in white letters designed to look like dripping paint.

"Are you the paperboy?" Robert Smith asks.

His lips are orangey red. His skin is as white as mine, but I believe he has applied powder, because I can see that it is caked in his nostril folds. He looks almost like the zombies that townies dress as on Halloween.

I stare at him. I am sure I am wide-eyed, as though he were the ghost, not I.

Is he your foster son, Mother and Father?

From the apartment comes music, a slow song featuring a sad violin and sung by a gloomy man who keeps repeating that he is always wishing for "impossible things."

Robert Smith repeats his question: "Is it collection day? You deliver the *Tribune*?"

I slowly shake my head. Then I say, "May I speak to Mr. and Mrs. Dalrymple?"

"Who?"

"The Dalrymples."

"Never heard of them."

He is not your foster son.

"They're barbers," I say. "They run Clippers out by the highway."

"You got the wrong building. All the buildings look alike in this sh*thole."

"The Dalrymples used to live in Apartment 6 at 222 Hill Drive. I am certain of that."

"Well, they don't no more. Me and my mom have been here three years now."

Oh dear! It never occurred to me you may have moved. I am unsure what to do. I hesitate. Robert Smith stares at me with his mascaraed eyes. Finally, I take a step forward. "May I come in and look around?" I ask.

On his middle finger, Robert Smith is wearing a silver ring with a skull engraving, a kind of death's head ring. I notice it because he reaches across the doorway to block my entry. He frowns his black eyebrows. "No, you little freak," he says. "You can't come in."

A boy in pancake makeup with bouffant hair is calling me a freak.

"Pretty please," I say.

Robert Smith slams the door.

98   [251.08]

Cf

Californium

AUTOMOBILES, TRUCKS, AND BUSES ZOOM ALONG THE HIGHWAY. They seem to move faster than they did thirteen years ago, but perhaps my memory is faulty, since the fastest thing in Town is a ten-speed bicycle. The vehicles zipping by also seem louder and dirtier than before. The exhaust they belch is stomach-turning; the honks they emit are earsplitting. Town may have its flaws, but at least the air is clean and the worst noise is a tone-deaf townie lying to himself that he can master the saxophone.

I stand at a crosswalk with two girls, both wearing striped wool sweaters unraveling at the waist, pink tutus(!), and thick-soled oxblood boots. One of the girls, the one with big eyeglasses, says to the other, "You're so bogus!"

Seeing the girl's glasses, I realize I still have my twenty-twenty vision. I wonder if you will recognize me without eyeglasses. What am I thinking? Of course you will. Will I recognize *you* is the question I should ask. You have aged thirteen years. Perhaps your hair is salt. Perhaps you are flabby, jowly, and wrinkly.

The light turns green, and I cross the highway. More fast-food joints have sprung up. Despite how garish the jumble of fluorescent signs is, I am awed. After all, heaven has no giant yellow sombreros advertising tacos and no giant dancing lobsters promoting seafood. The lobsters, I must say, seem overly happy for crustaceans that will be torn asunder and have their flesh sucked out of their claws.

The sidewalk here is no safer than before. The strip of lawn between it and the oncoming traffic is so thin a car could easily jump the curb and strike a person. I hope you always remain alert as you walk to work.

I spot a baseball cap lying in the grass. It is all blue except for a red letter *C* (the Chicago Cubs). I adjust the back strap and don the cap, pulling the visor down low. I should be an incognito ghost, just in case I bump into somebody who knows me.

Should I just walk into Clippers and say, "Hello there, Mother and Father"? You may accidentally jab your customers in the eyes with your scissors. Or faint and strike your heads so hard you get a concussion. Casper says it is now ten after four. Should I wait outside your shop till your customers leave? Will Zig give me enough haunting time?

An eighteen-wheeler roars past, beeping its horn. The noise is like an electric prod, and I start to run. I run at top speed till I reach the strip mall and then slow to a jog. I pass the druggist's, the pizza parlor, the pet shop, and the dry cleaner's, and I cannot believe my eyes. I stop dead in my tracks. Your barber pole is no longer there! The red and white stripes are gone. The blood and the bandages are a thing of the past.

Like a fifty-year-old townie, Clippers has vanished. *Poof!*

In its place stands a plant shop called Back to the Garden. I hurry to the window. Baskets of flowers have replaced your bottles of shampoos and hair tonics. Hung on the window is a poster of Adam and Eve, their bodies covered in vines. The sign reads, PLANTS: A GIFT THAT GROWS ON YOU. I press my nose against the glass and see an Asian man dressed in an apron who is selling a bouquet of gerberas to an old lady with lavender hair.

Where are you, dear Father and Mother?

There is a phone booth outside the pet shop. I trot back and leaf through the white pages. I find all the Dalrymples living in Cook County. Eight listings, but none of the names are yours or even Aunt Rose's. I flick through the yellow pages so wildly that

I rip a page in half. There is no Clippers among the barbershop listings.

I rest my forehead against the glass of the booth. "Help me, Zig," I whisper, my hope fading. "You brought me here. Tell me what to do."

I see a cat sleeping in the pet-shop window. A Siamese. Then I notice the shop's name on its front door.

In 1979, the pet shop was called Animal Lovers.

Today its name is Zoo.

Lordy! Lordy!

I hurry out of the phone booth and push open the shop's front door. A bell jingles, and the cat in the window lifts its sleepy head and throws me a look of ennui. Behind the cash register stands a young woman in a purple velour tracksuit. She is affixing discount stickers to boxes of birdseed and barely gives me a glance.

The name cannot be a coincidence, can it? I wander the aisles pondering what to do. The only customer in the store is an older teenager whose kneecaps stick out of big holes in his pale blue jeans. He is grimacing as he drags a hefty bag of dog kibble to the checkout counter.

I end up at the back of the shop in the rodent department, which smells strongly of wood chips. Shelves are stacked with terrariums of gerbils, hamsters, guinea pigs, rats, and mice. I drum my fingers against the glass of the mouse terrarium and eight pairs of nostrils sniff the air. The mice stare at me, beady-eyed and alarmed. As a ghost, I am only scary enough to give the willies to a litter of mice.

There are also tanks here containing tarantulas and lizards, and I notice a pair of beautiful geckos whose yellow bodies are covered with dark spots like a banana going mushy. Their little pink tongues dart in and out, reminding me of Pierre.

Another tank catches my eye. It is filled with insects crawling all over one another. Holy moly! They are death's head cockroaches! Dozens and dozens of *Blaberus craniifer*! I remember that this roach species is often used as lizard food.

Behind the wall of terrariums is a small area where employees tend the animals. Someone is there now. I see the person between the tanks. He is standing at a sink. His back is to me, but I see his dark ponytail, which extends to his shoulder blades. He is wearing khaki shorts and a sweatshirt.

The little hairs on the back of my neck go stiff.

I know this man.

He turns around and approaches the wall of tanks, lifts the wire-mesh lid of a terrarium, and drops in an empty paper-towel roll for the gerbils to chew apart.

Petrified, frozen in place, I watch the man. From somewhere in the shop, a parrot emits a loud squawk, and the cashier calls out, "Shut up, Aristotle!"

Johnny Henzel looks exactly the same as he does in Town. His hair is the same length, as is his beard. His cheekbones are just as sharp, his eyelashes just as dark. He even has the same pimple on his cheek.

He tried telling me the truth years ago. He was still in a coma here in America, he said. Rover was a bug, he claimed, but in the sense of a listening device that transmitted the voices of those around his hospital bed. Only *he* could hear those voices.

I did not believe him. He was a half-deader, but I thought him half-mad.

Patients in long comas often wake forgetting their past. Has Johnny forgotten his? Has he forgotten all about Town? All about me?

I step closer to the terrariums, my face between the gecko

tank and the lizard tank. I remove my Cubs cap and drop it on the floor.

Johnny has turned away from me. He takes a bag of rabbit pellets from a shelf and cuts it open with a pair of scissors.

I begin to hum a song, quietly at first and then louder.

The song is by Cole Porter, its lyrics a portmanteau.

Johnny puts down the pellets and turns slowly around. He knits his brow, creating the approximately-equal-to symbol ($\approx$) in the middle of his forehead.

He takes a few steps forward and stares at my face between the terrariums. His mouth falls open. His eyes go wide.

I stop humming. In a loud whisper, I say, "Boo!"

"I THOUGHT I WAS F*CKING CRAZY, MAN. LIKE MAYBE I DREAMT IT all up while I was comatose for all those months. Town, the Great Walls, Thelma and Esther, Zig, the death's head, the bricking."

Though still recognizable, Johnny's voice is much deeper than before. He and I are in the back room of Zoo, the door pushed half-closed. Beside us is a stack of cardboard boxes, and the bored-looking Siamese is now curled up atop them. Inside the boxes are tins of a cat food with an apt name: 9 Lives.

Johnny looks me up and down. "Man oh man, I can't believe you're here," he says. "It's so awesome, but also real f*cking freaky."

It is strange seeing him too. He is no longer the boy I knew. He is over six feet tall. He has a beard, which he keeps stroking. He is standing close and smells oniony, perhaps because he has no one here to remind him to shower.

"Where are my parents, Johnny?" I say, my voice squeaky. "I can find neither hide nor hair of them. I just stopped by 222 Hill Drive, but they are no longer there. A fellow with a powdered face lives in their apartment."

"Oh, jeez, your folks left years and years ago, back when I was in ninth grade. I heard they went to Alaska, but I'm not a hundred percent sure."

"Alaska!?" I cry. "I have serious doubts Zig will grant me enough haunting time for a trip to the largest state in the union."

The back room is furnished with a scratched desk that looks much like Johnny's old desk at the Frank and Joe. Scattered across the top are rubber chew toys for dogs: colorful bones, a plucked rooster, a great white shark. Beside the desk is a door to the outside propped open with, of all things, a brick.

"So you found a damn portal!" Johnny says.

"On my rebirthday, no less," I say. "Zig has granted me permission to visit you after all these years. But why now? I do not have the foggiest idea."

"I think I know." He pushes up the sleeves of his sweatshirt and holds his hands out palms up. Around both his wrists are flesh-colored bandages.

There is shame in his voice when he says, "I did a real stupid thing."

"Oh, Johnny, why would you do that?"

He smirks at me. "Once a sadcon, always a sadcon."

I touch one of the bandages with the tip of my finger. I know what lies beneath: the same ugly scars are on his wrists back in Town. It dawns on me that his doppelgänger at Curios probably started aging on the day Johnny sliced through his veins here in America.

"My shrink has me on anti-sadcon pills, but the f*cking things don't always work."

He gives me a searching look. "You'll think I'm nuts, but sometimes I miss Town. Sometimes I put my ear against my tank of roaches, hoping I'll hear voices from Town. Maybe even you talking to me again, correcting my grammar."

I do not mention his twin at Curios lest I frighten him. "You can never go back, Johnny," I say with finality.

He nods his head, looking a little morose, but then he brightens. "Man, you're so young!" he exclaims. "Or I'm so old. I don't know which. You're just a little kid. In my mind, I remembered you older."

"I am older than I used to be in the mental sense, but of course not in the physical."

"Whereas I'm old and I'm mental," he says, and lets out a guffaw.

Though his joke is macabre, I do crack a smile.

"I've missed you, man." He reaches out and gently ruffles my staticky hair the way you used to, Father. "You saved me, Boo. You saved my life. And now here you are again when I need you most."

The Siamese meows as if agreeing with Johnny. Its eyes are the same sky blue as mine.

"You're a sign," Johnny says.

"Of what?"

"Of life," he says. "The life I'm supposed to hang on to."

Should I finally ask why he shot me?

Perhaps it is best that I not know.

We are standing near a bulletin board, and a photo thumbtacked to it catches my eye: Johnny with Zoo's cashier. They wear matching T-shirts, the word NIRVANA written across the chest. Below the word is a kind of smiley face, but the eyes are X's and the mouth is squiggly. Above their heads Johnny and the girl hold large signs. His reads GRAND; hers reads OPENING.

"Is that your sister?" I ask.

"Yeah, Brenda's the only one I told about Town. I said the place was probably just some weird, psychedelic dream, but she was like, 'No, no, Johnny. You died and that's where you went.' She believed even when I had trouble believing."

"There is a family resemblance," I say. "You have the same coppery eyes. Also the same dimple in your left cheek."

"Oh, I have to introduce you two. She'll frigging flip out. Stay put, okay? I'll be right back."

Johnny pushes the door open and heads into Zoo. I can hear a customer talking loudly to Brenda about Zig knows what. "Are you sure it clumps?" the lady says. "I need it to clump. And it's gotta flush. It's gotta flush *and* clump."

Taped to the opposite wall of the back room are dozens of photographs of Johnny and Brenda. I cross the floor for a better look. My eyes dart here and there, seeing Johnny throughout his life. A prom-goer in a baby blue tuxedo with his arm around an older Cynthia Orwell. A seventh-grade track star with a gold medal around his neck. A young driver sitting at the wheel of a convertible, a basset hound beside him in the passenger's seat. A squinting bearded artist standing beside a swirling abstract mural painted on a brick wall.

Then I see this photo: a hollow-eyed eighth grader sitting up in bed, his head in bandages. Johnny is clutching a heart-shaped throw cushion. Stitched across the heart is a single word: HERO.

An odd gift for a boy who shot another.

"I have customers, Johnny," Brenda says out in Zoo. "Your surprise can't wait?"

I turn around as Johnny and his sister walk into the back room. They stop in the doorway.

Johnny grins wildly.

Brenda frowns. "Customers aren't allowed back here," she says. Then her frown vanishes, and she gapes at me.

"No, no," she whispers. "No freaking way."

"Yes freaking way," Johnny replies.

Brenda takes a few steps forward, one arm outstretched. She wants to touch me, I think. She wants to see whether her hand passes right through.

"He's solid," Johnny says.

"Hello, Brenda Henzel," I say, backing against the wall. "You have certainly matured since last we met."

A strangled whimper escapes her mouth. Her arm drops to her side. Her eyes roll backward. Her knees buckle, and she falls hard, slapping against the concrete floor.

"Dear me," I say to the heap of purple velour.

Johnny hurries over. "Sh*t, sh*t, sh*t," he mutters as he goes down on his knees to help his sister.

"She experienced a drop in the amount of blood flow to her brain," I say to explain why a person faints.

Johnny turns Brenda faceup and gently pats her cheek. She is as white as a sliced potato, except for a red mark at her hairline where her head must have bounced off the concrete.

"Have any smelling salts?" I ask, standing over them.

"Smelling salts?" Johnny says. "What the f*ck's that?"

"Ammonia carbonate."

The chemical formula is $(NH_4)_2CO_3$, but I do not say so because now is not the time.

"The only ammonia I got here is Windex," Johnny says, his voice shriller.

Brenda flutters her eyelids and emits a groan. The Siamese jumps down from its 9 Lives and sniffs her scalp.

"Perhaps I should skedaddle," I say. "She may black out again if she comes to and sees a ghost hovering."

Johnny gives me a look of regret. "But where'll you go?"

"Back home. Back to Town."

"How'll you get there, Boo?"

Like a religious fanatic, I say, "Zig will show me the way."

I undo my Casper the Friendly Ghost wristwatch and hand it over as a souvenir. "So you will always remember the time," I say.

I mean not only this moment in time, but also our time together in Town.

Johnny's mouth is smiling, but his eyes still look somewhat doleful. "As if I would've forgot," he says.

" 'Forgotten,' " I correct.

Then Brenda opens her eyes, focuses on my face, and screams blue murder.

100 [257.10]

Fm

Formium

AFTER I BOLT AWAY FROM ZOO, I DRIFT THROUGH THE VAST stretches of bungalows that populate Hoffman Estates. On one street, a little girl about seven years old asks if I would like a before-dinner mint. She is standing at the end of her driveway with a fake tiara on her head. In her hand, she has a hard candy wrapped in green cellophane. I am touched by her kindness, particularly since Zig does not give us townies candy.

A little later, as I am sucking on the mint, I step into the road without looking both ways and nearly get clipped by a station wagon. "Watch it, goofball!" the driver yells. I realize I am now on Meadow Lane, the street where Johnny and I once lay in the snow to watch the heavens.

I meander around Sandpits for a while. Have you gone to Anchorage, dear Mother and Father? When we sailed to Alaska, we all expressed a wish to move there one day. Are you in the land of the moose? Without your presence here, Sandpits no longer holds much appeal, so I vamoose and head toward Helen Keller.

As I cross the long field that stretches out behind the school, I feel a queasiness in my gut. I do not understand my reaction until, in the yellowing grass, I spot an empty can of cola lying on its side. I stop in my tracks. I recall that this is the field where Kevin Stein, Nelson Bliss, and Henry Axworthy attacked me with stones on the first day of eighth grade.

I also remember something I had forgotten.

After my attackers threw their rocks and I fell to the ground stunned and bleeding, they stood over me and made a pact. Pig-nosed Kevin held his hand to his heart and put on a solemn voice. "I pledge to make every day of this school year a living hell for Oliver 'Boo' Dalrymple," he said. Nelson repeated the line, and so did Henry. Then, the three of them together cried, "One nation under God, amen!"

There was an empty can of pop lying nearby. Lemon soda. Kevin picked up the can. Then he unzipped the fly of his jeans and fished around for his penis. He did not turn away. He dared me to watch. I closed my eyes, but I could hear him. He was urinating into the pop can. The sound was like liquid being poured into a beaker.

"Hold him down," he told Nelson and Henry, who then sat on my arms.

I told myself it did not matter: after all, it was mostly water with traces of inorganic salts and organic compounds. *Relax and just swallow,* I told myself. Yet I did not surrender quietly this time. I fought. I screamed. I tried hooking my legs around my assailants to knock them off. I did not manage, though. Nelson's grimy fingers wrenched my mouth open, and Kevin poured the warm urine down my throat. I sputtered and choked. It went up my bloody nose, all over my face, in my hair, and even in my ears.

They won. They would always win.

How strange that I am recalling this now.

It is a memory that Zig found fit to erase.

For thirteen years, this memory lay in a kind of vault. Also in there was the despair I felt. It comes back to me now. Even after they left me, I remained lying in this field for an hour or two. Drained. Forlorn. Beaten.

Now, in the distance, a half dozen kids run screaming across the same field. Whether they are terrorizing one another or just playing I cannot tell. A robin lands a yard away. It stares at me, head tilted one way and then the other, as though I am a tricky puzzle it is trying to solve.

"Hello, angel," I say to the bird.

It flies away, and then I walk over to the empty can of pop. I jump up and down on the thing till it is good and flat. Then I pick it up and wing it across the field like a Frisbee.

I head back to the long brick school that is Helen Keller. I worry its doors may be locked because it is now suppertime. Will I need to break in? But no, the doors are open, and a few boys mill around in the lobby. They are dressed in what look like pajamas but are actually judo uniforms tied with orange belts. They pay me no mind. I walk down the hall past show cases with sports trophies locked behind glass.

Johnny won track-and-field trophies for Helen Keller in seventh grade. I expect, however, that he was not allowed to complete eighth grade here. Which school did he attend instead? A kind of reform school, I imagine.

Zig permitted this haunting, I suppose, to show me that Johnny has managed to carry on with his life, even though certain ghosts haunt him still. I am one of those ghosts. Perhaps I helped him today. I dearly hope so.

When I reach my old locker, I see that No. 106 is padlocked. I assume I know the combination: I turn the dial to 7, to 25, and then to 34. I yank the lock and it opens.

I check behind me, but no one is around. Only Helen Keller's eyes watch from across the hall.

I squeak the door open, expecting the rear panel to be missing and the locker to be empty. But the panel is in place and the locker full. The objects in it, though, do not belong to the Asian girl I met earlier in the hallway. Holy moly, they belong to me!

My periodic table is taped to the back of the door. Above it are my photos of Jane Goodall and Richard Dawkins. Jane with her sleek blond ponytail and her pursed lips. Richard with his impish grin and his unruly eyebrows. "Hello there, hello," I say. "You two look good. You have not aged a single day."

My compass and protractor set is in my locker, as are my chemistry and mathematics textbooks. My school copy of *Lord of the Flies*, its spine still unbroken. My forest green cardigan sweater that Grandmother gave me for my thirteenth birthday. My French-English dictionary. My cracked-vinyl gym bag with my gym clothes still inside: yellow shorts, Trojan T-shirt, even a jockstrap.

I riffle through my belongings. At the back of the top shelf is a paper bag. I assume it is the lunch you made me thirteen years ago, Mother and Father. I pull it toward me. It is heavy. Heavier than a peanut butter sandwich, a granola bar, and a box of raisins should be.

I open the paper bag.

Inside is a revolver.

Not the one from Curios.

Uncle Seymour's gun.

I glance up. Helen Keller stares at me from her wall. She nods her mortarboard head. At least in my mind she does.

Then I remember.

Me aiming this gun at my own chest. Johnny yelling, *"No!"* Throwing himself at me. The panic in his eyes. The scars on his wrists. The wrenching and the wrestling. The loud bang.

101 [258.10]
Md
Mendelevium

HYDROGEN, HELIUM, LITHIUM, BERYLLIUM, BORON, CARBON, nitrogen, oxygen, fluorine, neon, sodium, magnesium, aluminum, silicon, phosphorus, sulfur, chlorine, argon, potassium, calcium, scandium, titanium, vanadium, chromium, manganese, iron, cobalt, nickel, copper, zinc, gallium, germanium, arsenic, selenium, bromine, krypton, rubidium, strontium, yttrium, zirconium, niobium, molybdenum, technetium, ruthenium, rhodium, palladium, silver, cadmium, indium, tin, antimony, tellurium, iodine, xenon, cesium, barium, lanthanum, cerium, praseodymium, neodymium, promethium, samarium, europium, gadolinium, terbium, dysprosium, holmium, erbium, thulium, ytterbium, lutetium, hafnium, tantalum, tungsten, rhenium, osmium, iridium, platinum, gold, mercury, thallium, lead, bismuth, polonium, astatine, radon, francium, radium, actinium, thorium, protactinium, uranium, neptunium, plutonium, americium, curium, berkelium, californium, einsteinium, fermium, mendelevium, nobelium, lawrencium, rutherfordium, dubnium, seaborgium, bohrium, hassium, meitnerium.

102   [259.10]

No

Nobelium

I CURL MYSELF INTO NO. 106 AND SLAM THE DOOR. I AM SWALLOWED by darkness. I am cramped, sweaty, shaky. I gasp for breath. There is a paper bag in my hand, but I cannot use it for CO_2. I let it go, and the gun clunks at my feet. I start weeping quietly, and the sleeves of my cardigan sweater hang around me like an embrace. This locker is my coffin. May I never leave it.

Time creeps along. I cannot tell how much time. Twenty minutes? Two hours? But eventually the locker's back panel is tugged open, and before me stands a boy with a Mohawk stiffened with white glue (polyvinyl acetate). "Jesus!" he cries. "You almost gave me a heart attack!"

When I unfold myself and slip out of the locker, I feel lifeless. I am a zombie. The walking dead. The warehouse is now filled with dozens of sorters rummaging through the delivered goods and piling items into buggies and onto dollies. They are as diligent as worker ants.

"What were you doing in there?" the punk rocker asks.

"Looking for unusual finds," I mutter.

"There's nothing unusual about this beat-up locker."

"Au contraire," I reply.

I glance back inside the locker. It is empty once again. All my belongings are gone, including the paper bag. I close the locker door.

I arrange for the punk rocker to deliver No. 106 to Curios later in the week. I ask him the time now, and he says five to eleven. I was away for several hours.

I pick up my rock-filled flashlight and shuffle back to the Guy Montag Library. Coming up the library's walkway, I hear a yapping, and Pierre clambers out of the bushes that grow alongside the building. Heavens, I had forgotten all about the dog. He leaps up and down to welcome me back. I carry him inside. When we reach Curios on the third floor, I am hesitant to enter, but I force myself to undo the chain lock. My footsteps echo and Pierre's nails clickety-clack as we walk through the exhibit halls. Despite the dozens of displays, the space feels empty, as though not a soul is around. I say to Pierre, "Let's see if his soul is still here."

We head to Johnny's room, and I drag the armoire away from his door. When I go inside, I am not shocked to find the bed empty. Lying atop it are red gym shorts, a white tank top, and a blue bauble. I slip the items into the drawer underneath the bed where the revolver still resides.

Just in case, I check to see whether Zig filled the gun with bullets during my absence, but there are none inside. Well, I guess I cannot shoot myself in my stupid brain or defective heart.

I doff my T-shirt and jeans and climb under the covers in only my shorts. A slight whiff of onions lingers. Pierre hops onto the bed and curls up at my feet. I am very, very tired, yet I wonder whether I will ever fall asleep again, and if I do, will I ever wake?

My voice trembles slightly when, to the ceiling fan, I say, "Tell me a bedtime story, Zig. But please, no more fairy tales. No more fiction."

The ceiling fan whirls and twirls.

"I want the truth."

As usual, Zig says nothing. But he does not need to reply. I now know the truth. I know in my holey heart what you, dear Mother and Father, have long known: your son was Gunboy.

PLEASE.

104	[267.12]
Rf	
Rutherfordium	

PLEASE.

105	[268.13]
Db	
Dubnium	

FORGIVE ME.

SEVEN WEEKS HAVE PASSED, MOTHER AND FATHER, AND DURING this time, I have told not a soul but you about my haunting and the mysteries it unraveled. To keep my sanity, I have kept busy. I have revamped Curios. Let me share with you an exhibition I have designed called *Curiouser and Curiouser*. Esther suggested the title, which comes from *Alice's Adventures in Wonderland*, a fictional book I intend to read one day.

Tonight is the grand reopening of Curios. In the past weeks, I moved every object in the museum's collection into basement storage at the library. Down went our dollar coins, Chinese kite, batteries, out-of-order phones, personal computer (a new arrival), condoms, diapers, *Encyclopaedia Britannica* Volume Ma to Mi, roll-on deodorant, pet terrariums, animal replicas, corned beef, boxes of Hamburger Helper, lucky rabbit's foot, ceramic statue of Jesus's supposedly virgin mother, wallaby postal stamps from Australia, and on and on.

As for the little revolver, I threw it down the garbage chute. It is gone forever. Or perhaps not forever, because for all I know Zig may boomerang it back one day.

After I moved all the curiosities downstairs, I began traveling to Town's infirmaries, which, over the years, have all received photocopiers from Zig's warehouse deliveries. I spent day after day photocopying the documents I planned to display as part of *Curiouser and Curiouser*.

Tonight is October 31. As on every Halloween, I simply throw a white sheet over my head. Through its eyeholes, I can gauge the reactions of my visitors, who come as zombies, witches, mummies, monsters, archangels, goblins, and the like. They come with their fake blood and gore. They come with fake arrows through their heads. They come with fake knives sticking out of their backs. These dead children walk around the halls of my museum in wonder. I cannot always see their wonder under their masks and makeup, but I can sense it.

There are no displays tonight as such. Instead, the actual walls are the exhibits. I have divided the museum into thirteen areas, each identified by a large number painted its own distinct color on bristol board. Using simple gluc sticks, I wallpapered the walls with photocopies of every page of the surviving rebirthing books from the thirteen infirmaries. On these pages are listed newborns' names, the city they came from, the date of their rebirth, the cause of their passing, and the zip code of their assigned address. Most of the pages are typewritten, but the oldest books (I found one dating back to 1938) are handwritten, the ink so faded it is often illegible. The pages run chronologically in a horizontal fashion across the walls, the oldest in the top left corner, the newest in the bottom right corner.

Curiouser and Curiouser is a memorial to everyone who has ever come to Town. My aim is for each of my fellow townies to feel he or she is a beautiful, curious object.

I did not know how people would react. Would they be impressed? Bored? It appears the former is the case. They are reading the documents as though they are pages from a fascinating novel. Council president Reginald Washington (a pirate) is here, as are jail warden Lydia Finkle (a witch), asylum manager Dr. Albert Schmidt (a ghoul), and former Schaumburg resident Sandy Goldberg (a giant felt peanut).

The irksome twins Tim and Tom Lu come as well, wearing fake mustaches and carrying canes. They are dressed as Thompson and Thomson from *Tintin*.

Tim says to Tom, "I wonder if after all these years Oliver Dalrymple is still the victim."

"Would it were true," I reply.

Like many other visitors, Tim and Tom climb the stepladders placed in the halls to search for their own names on the rebirthing lists. Meanwhile, Pierre weaves in and out of people's legs and yaps like a mad dog and, when egged on, does his *wee-ooo-wee-ooo*.

My friends are here too. Thelma is dressed as Sherlock Holmes in a tweed deerstalker, Esther as a gypsy medium in a headscarf decorated with signs of the zodiac, and Ringo as a mummy wrapped in white bandages stained with fake blood.

Ringo's costume reminds me of your old red-and-white barber's pole, Father and Mother. Did you take it with you to Alaska? I do not know for sure you went there, but I do like thinking of you mingling with bears and moose in downtown Anchorage and admiring the aurora borealis at night.

I tell my friends to meet me in Johnny's room. I have a toast to make. I go to my office and, from my bottom desk drawer, fetch a bottle of a French red wine called Château Bel-Air, which came to Town in 1977. I conceal it, with plastic glasses and a corkscrew, in a wicker picnic basket.

When I arrive in Johnny's room, the section of the exhibition I reserved for the reborn children of Eleven, my three friends are waiting with Pierre, who, if he *is* from Paris, is perhaps familiar with Château Bel-Air (ha-ha). I tell any other visitors to clear out for a moment because I have vital business to attend to. Once the others are gone, I close the door and press its push lock.

I show my friends what is in the picnic basket. Ringo, who claims to have been a virtual wino back in Detroit, says, "That's bloody fantastic, mate!" Esther, Thelma, and I have never tasted wine before. I ask Ringo to do the honors, and he clenches the bottle between his bandaged thighs and deftly threads the screw into the cork. He yanks out the cork with a sound like the pop of a pistol. We all sit in the middle of the floor as though in a powwow. I fill the glasses halfway and pass them around.

Thelma gets giggly even before taking a sip. "Reginald better not find out. We'll get detention for a year."

I raise my glass and say, "A toast to Johnny Henzel."

My friends raise their glasses. The girls both give me nervous grins. We rarely speak about Johnny nowadays. Maybe Esther and Thelma made a pact long ago to avoid mentioning him in front of me. Or perhaps they just stopped thinking about him years ago and are embarrassed they have forgotten all about their old friend.

"He was born in America on Halloween," I add.

"To Johnny Henzel," they all say, clinking glasses.

I like to think that Johnny's stay in Town was no mistake. Zig *wanted* him in Town, at least for a little while, so we could become friends, the fast friends we should have been in our earthly lives. Had we been best friends back then, Johnny might not have slashed his wrists and I might not have stolen Uncle Seymour's gun. We could have helped each other in America the way we helped each other in the sweet hereafter.

My friends sip their wine. I lack a mouth hole in my costume, so I must raise my glass beneath the sheet to drink. The wine is warm and syrupy.

Esther says, "This stuff tastes better than I expected."

Thelma says, "It tastes like adulthood."

"It tastes nutmeggy," Ringo says. He inspects the label on the bottle. "Seventy-seven was an ace year."

"Nutmeggy?" Esther rolls her eyes.

Ringo gulps from his glass. Then he says, "So where the hell's Johnny boy?"

"Is he cooped up in the basement?" Esther asks.

I shake my head. "He flew the coop."

Esther and Thelma lift their eyebrows. Thelma then holds up her Sherlock Holmes magnifying glass as though to examine the ghost before her more closely.

"He re-redied," I clarify.

"I'll be damned!" Ringo cries.

Thelma puts down her magnifying glass. "He vanished?"

"Poof!" I say.

"When?" Esther asks.

"On the seventh of September," I say. I do not mention Johnny turning into Town's first man. I am not ready for full disclosure at the moment. One day, perhaps.

"Cripes, Boo!" Esther says. "You should have told us!"

"We could have held a funeral," Thelma says. "We could have honored him."

"I honored him for thirteen years," I say from beneath my sheet. "Maybe that was enough."

Thelma pats my ghost head. "You hunky-dory?"

"Not really." I take a big gulp from my wine, which warms my belly.

Ringo asks if I organized *Curiouser and Curiouser* as a distraction from my mourning. "Keep your mind off things?" he says.

I nod, even though I am not sure this is true. I do not know if I have been mourning Johnny Henzel. Maybe I have been. He was, after all, a kind of hero to me. But the person I have really been mourning is Oliver Dalrymple.

The boy I thought I was but was not.

My friends and I drink the rest of the bottle of wine. Ringo keeps saying, "Feel anything? Feel anything?" as though we are on the verge of becoming whole different people.

But I am already a whole different person.

My friends giggle when they notice that their teeth are stained purple. I swallow my last gulp of wine and stand. I am dizzy and queasy but a bit hunkier-dorier. I go to the wall where Johnny's bed once was. I wave my friends over to see a page from the infirmary in Eleven. It is pasted in the middle of the wall. Esther must stand on tippytoe.

"I typed that up," Thelma says about the page.

"Your spelling is atrocious," Ringo says.

These are the first entries on the page:

Kendra Phillips	Murray, UT	5 July 79	lukemia	TIP
Nick Easterling	Tewksbury, MA	17 July 79	fell out of tree fort	BAG
Haley Pierson-Cox	Louisville, CO	28 July 79	pnamonia	LOT
Jane Brunk	Vienna, VA	31 July 79	hit by bus	HAM
Lisa Antonopoulos	Sherwood, OR	22 Aug. 79	smoke inalation	PAT

A dozen entries down, this is how the page ends:

| Oliver Dalrymple | Hoffman Estates, IL | 7 Sept. 79 | holy heart | GUT |
| John Henzel | Hoffman Estates, IL | 12 Oct. 79 | bullet in brain | GUT |

I point to my cause of death. I tell my friends that I think the hole in my heart has finally closed over. "I can't feel it twinging anymore," I say. "I don't know if this is good news."

Esther's zodiac scarf has slipped down, and the scorpion

seems about to pinch her nose with its claws. She says, "It's good news, Boo."

Thelma agrees: "It means you've healed."

"Thirteen years is a long time to heal," I reply. "In my healing ledger, it is record-breaking."

"Too bad that people down in America don't heal fast," Thelma says. "Like our moms and dads and sisters and brothers after we passed. If only their hearts healed lickety-split."

We all think of our families and get a little blue, perhaps because we are blotto—a word you liked to use to describe yourselves whenever you drank dry martinis after work.

Mother and Father, I now keep locker No. 106 in my office and occasionally check inside to see if it opens onto another world. So far, no, but perhaps one day there will appear an Alaskan barbershop. Inside the locker, I store the book I have written, which is ready and waiting for delivery. I will hand it to you and then retreat back to my world, and you will read my story and finally understand the nitty-gritty of my life and afterlife. Afterward, you will close my book and lay me to rest, and my ghost will no longer haunt you.

Esther interrupts everybody's reveries. "Let's not be sad and confused tonight," she says.

I tell my friends there is a second bottle of wine in my office. A bottle of white wine from the Napa Valley.

"Oh, go get it!" Ringo cries. "We can get sh*tfaced and then go to that big Halloween do in the Northeast Corner." He is sparkly-eyed beneath his bandages. "Let's go wild and crazy tonight!" He does a cartwheel across the room, a miracle given his costume and his bellyful of wine. Pierre barks and bounces up and down on his woolly legs. Ringo scoops the dog up and does a pogo dance with Pierre in his arms.

"Can you go wild and crazy, Estie?" Ringo shouts to Esther.

"You better believe it." Esther bounces on her toes.

"What about you, Thelma?"

"Lordy, yes."

"And you, Boo? Can you go wild and crazy?"

I mull the question over.

"There is a distinct possibility," I say.

ACKNOWLEDGMENTS

Many thanks to Paul Taunton at Knopf Canada and Lexy Bloom at Vintage Books in New York, and to Dean Cooke, Ron Eckel, and Suzanne Brandreth at the Cooke Agency. Additional thanks to Jessica Grant, Ross Rogers, David Posel, Lois Carson, and Frank Smith. *Un gros merci à Christian Dorais.*